To
Mr. Rahman from TAROC
July 11th 1990.

[signatures]

REFLECTIONS OF
TAIWAN

ACKNOWLEDGEMENTS
The following people contributed invaluable assistance
and advice in the production of this book:-
Mickey Chen, Teddy Chen, Margaret Cheong,
Chia Yue-Puo, Mary Crawley, Robert Ducas, Colin Gatenby,
Hwang Ching-Hwai, David Lee, Li Kun-kun, Joan Lloyd,
William Lue Hsi-Ming, Robin Moyer, Jack H.Y. Niu,
Rina Segal, Molly Sung, Tan Bee Choo, Sylvia Tan,
Nellie Tung Nai-Cha, Mike Workman, Yu Wei.
    Most of all we would like to thank the people of Taiwan
for providing "the flavor of human feeling" which lies
at the heart of Chinese culture in Taiwan.

Photographs in this book are available for re-use for magazines, brochures
and advertising etc. from the library of R.Ian Lloyd Productions Pte. Ltd.
11th Flr Inchcape House, 450/452 Alexandra Road, Singapore 0511
Tel: 475 2033   Telex: RS 50634 LLOYD   Fax: 472 1690

Typesetting by Koford Prints Pte. Ltd.
Color separations by Daiichi Process Pte. Ltd.
Printed in Singapore by Toppan Printing Pte. Ltd.

ISBN No. 9971-84-897-X
First edition 1987

Distributed in Taiwan by Caves Books, Ltd.
103 Chung Shan N. Road, Sec. 2, Taipei, Taiwan R.O.C.
Tel: 537-1666/541-4754

REFLECTIONS OF
TAIWAN

PHOTOGRAPHY BY R. IAN LLOYD · TEXT BY DANIEL P. REID

Edited by Derek A.C. Davies · Translations by Patrick Y.S. Yang
Designed by Viscom Design Associates

Published by R. Ian Lloyd Productions Pte. Ltd.

The author and photographer wish to thank the following organizations
and companies, whose generous support and encouragement
helped make the publication of this book possible:

National Chiang Kai-shek Cultural Center R.O.C.
National Theater · National Concert Hall

Government Information Office of the Republic of China

Tourism Bureau, Ministry of Communications, the Republic of China

Taipei International Convention Center

Hilton International Taipei

Caves Books Ltd.

Asia Chemical Corp.
Crown Van Lines International Movers
Howard Plaza Hotel
International Engineering & Construction Corp.
Investec (Taiwan) Ltd.
Maritime Transportation Agencies, Ltd.
Orient Pacific International Mover's
Taiwan Hung Lau Enterprise Ltd.
Taiwan Polypropylene Co., Ltd.
U.S. Shoe Far East Ltd
Westinghouse Electric S.A. Taiwan Branch

In order to pacify the world,
    The sage first pacifies his nation.
In order to pacify the nation,
    The sage first pacifies his family.
In order to pacify his family,
    The sage first cultivates his character.
In order to cultivate his character,
    The sage first regulates his mind.
In order to regulate his mind,
    He must first purify his heart.

CONFUCIUS

*I*lha Formosa — "The Beautiful Island."

So the Portuguese mariners who "discovered" Taiwan as they sailed from Macao to Japan named it in 1590; and so it remained known to the Western world until the mid-twentieth century. Unlike the barren island of Hong Kong ceded to Britain by the Chinese emperor in the wake of the Opium Wars, Formosa stood as a beacon of wealth and beauty at the hub of the trade routes between Shanghai, Korea, and Japan to the north and Hong Kong, Macao, and the Philippines to the south. Britian, Portugal, Spain, Holland, America, and Japan all cast envious eyes on The Beautiful Island and each in turn plotted to possess her, but in the end she settled down with her most courteous and cultured suitor, China.

Early Chinese settlers called her by another name — *Bao Dao*, or "Treasure Island." Taiwan's soil was rich and fecund, her mountains thick with camphor, cedar, and other precious woods, and her valleys lush with the indispensable lifeblood of water.

At first the settlers from the mainland came as a trickle: marauding pirates seeking refuge from the law, minority Hakkas escaping ethnic persecution, enterprising traders in search of profit. But during the seventeenth century, when the Manchus swept down from the north in their relentless campaign to topple and supplant the Ming Dynasty, that trickle became a flood of exodus. Under Koxinga, a Chinese pirate-turned-patriot who made a valiant last stand against the Manchus on the mainland, Taiwan became a bastion of resistance to Manchu usurpers in Peking, a role she would play again three hundred years later as the island fortress of the Republic of China in its simmering dispute with communist rivals on the mainland.

The name Taiwan, which means "Terraced Bay" in Chinese, was coined by the seafaring eunuch Cheng Ho around 1430, when he claimed the island on behalf of the Ming emperor during his overseas naval explorations. But some scholars believe that the term is a corruption of "Paiwan," which is the name of a major and once powerful aboriginal tribe that still inhabits the southern regions of the island where the Chinese first settled.

Despite its colorful history and seductive allure, Taiwan remains an enigma to most Westerners, many of whom continue to confuse it with Thailand. ("So you live in Taiwan,"

say my friends back home. "I hear Bangkok is a great town!")

The main reason for Taiwan's international obscurity is political: most countries have severed formal relations with the Republic of China on Taiwan, leaving the island in diplomatic limbo. But its economic strength also creates a misleading or incomplete image. Though no bigger than Holland, Taiwan today boasts the world's fastest growing economy and second largest container port and ranks as the world's fourteenth greatest trading power. When people think of Taiwan, they usually think of textiles and tennis rackets, shoes and socket wrenches, canned mushrooms and cloned computers, not majestic mountains and verdant valleys, ancient temples and traditional culture.

Even a visit to Taiwan often fails to bring the island into proper perspective, especially when one comes here exclusively to do business, as do about seventy per cent of all foreign visitors, and spends all one's time in Taipei city. Unless you prepare yourself with some preliminary historical and cultural background on China, or know a few "old Taiwan hands" living on the island, a trip to Taiwan can be about as memorable as a stopover in an airport transit lounge.

Those who come to Taiwan as traders or tourists rather than intrepid travelers will get precisely what they bargained for: a good deal on a line of manufactured products, or a whirlwind sightseeing and shopping tour conducted from the insulation of an air-conditioned bus. But those who take to heart the ancient Chinese adage, "When entering a foreign land, follow the local customs," will find Taiwan to be a kaleidoscope of colorful contrasts between old and new, traditional and modern, East and West, and a treasure trove of classical Chinese culture. From the graceful sweep of tiled temple eaves to the tubular thrust of modern skyscrapers, from the timeless patterns of Chinese agriculture to the latest frontiers of high-tech industry, Taiwan sparkles with clear reflections of the world's most ancient civilization as it forges full speed ahead into the modern world. Those who are willing to leave their own cultural biases behind and "stretch out a hand" will indeed discover that the Chinese in Taiwan have a gift to give them.

That gift is a curious blend of friendship and frankness, tact and fact, candor and culture, which is exquisitely expressed in the Chinese language as *ren-ching-wei,* literally "the flavor of human feeling." It's a spicey flavor long forgotten in the blandly scientific societies of the West, where logic and legality all too often erode the emotional moorings of family and friendship that have always been so important to the Chinese and continue to lie at the heart of life in Taiwan today. The Chinese flavour of human feeling which suffuses life in Taiwan is every bit as satisfying to the heart as Chinese food is to the stomach; but while traditional Chinese food is now available throughout the world, traditional Chinese feeling has become a rare dish best sampled in Taiwan.

On a map, Taiwan looks like a bright green leaf floating in the clear blue waters of the East China Sea, only a short sail from her mammoth mainland neighbor. On the island itself, much of Taiwan looks like a miniature replica of fabled Chinese scenes, complete with pine-studded peaks and cascading waterfalls, sunny seashores and shadey lakes, as well as the requisite pavilion or pagoda, corniced wall or temple gate perfectly placed in the background to enhance rather than dominate the natural setting.

According to Chinese legend, Taiwan was formed by a playful sea dragon who tossed massive rocks up from beneath the sea with tremulous gyrations and fiery breath. Figuratively, this accords well with the theory of modern geologists, who say that the island was created by powerful volcanoes and earthquakes, which pushed it up from the ocean floor. Coral deposits can be found in the igneous rocks of Taiwan's mountains as high as two thousand feet above sea level, which substantiates the island's draconian volcanic birth.

Mountains are the island's major geological feature, covering over two-thirds of its land area with rugged peaks draped in a lush blend of alpine and tropical foliage. People who never venture beyond the capital, Taipei, miss out on one of Asia's most beautiful mountain ranges,

the great Central Range, whose towering ridges bisect Taiwan from north to south and include Northeast Asia's tallest peak, Jade Mountain, 13,113 feet above sea level.

Mountains are also the abode of Taiwan's "mountain people," which is what the Chinese call the island's indigenous aboriginal tribes. Currently numbering about a quarter of a million, Taiwan's aborigines have been here for well over ten thousand years, and nine tribes still maintain their ancient traditions in isolated communities scattered throughout the Central Range. As talented musicians, dancers, weavers, and carvers, the aborigines add colorful threads to the tapestry of Taiwan.

While the *yang* element of fire gave birth to the island, the *yin* element of water nurtures it, forms its character, and occasionally beats it silly with violent tantrums known as "typhoons." If anything in the world can make a person renew his respect for the raw power of nature and the awesome forces of wind and water, it's a Taiwan typhoon.

Water appears in many different guises in Taiwan. Most obvious is the island's natural legacy of saltwater beaches. Then there is rain, which accounts for an average of forty-five inches of water throughout the island every year, with four or five times that amount falling on the higher reaches of the Central Range. This rainfall forms short, swift rivers which occasionally flood the lowlands and feed magnificent waterfalls that enliven the landscape. Elsewhere, water forms idyllic lakes, such as Taiwan's favorite honeymoon resort, Sun Moon Lake.

As it sinks deep into the island's simmering volcanic fissures, water is heated to a boil by the "dragon's breath," impregnated with vital minerals from the earth, then percolated back up to the surface as soothing, therapeutic hot springs, which constitute one of the island's most attractive features. Over one hundred hot spring sources bubble their healing, sulphorous mineral waters up from the earth throughout the island, but only about a dozen have been developed into fully-fledged spas.

The most pervasive and potent form of water in Taiwan is the invisible yet palpable shroud of humidity that envelopes the entire island throughout the year. Never dropping below eighty percent, this penetrating cloak of airborne moisture intensifies the heat of summer and exagger-

ates the chill of winter. This invisible yet ever-present water gives Taiwan's climate its distinctively feminine character and makes the island's weather so unpredictable. Within the course of a single day, temperatures can vary as much as twenty degrees Fahrenheit. You may awaken enshrouded by clouds and haze in the morning, enjoy clear sunny skies by noon, get drenched by afternoon thundershowers, then shiver in the evening chill.

Such an unpredictable and changeable climate seems to intensify human emotions and brings out the distinctive "flavor of human feeling" that characterizes the traditional Chinese society in Taiwan. Sometimes Mother Nature envelopes Taiwan in a heady haze of heat and humidity that saps the energy and debilitates the bodies of its inhabitants, turning the whole island into a huge sauna. Strange moods and odd cravings grip the islanders on such days, especially in the steamy asphalt jungles of Taipei. Cafes and tea rooms, barber shops and bath houses, and other air-conditioned oases of comfort do a brisk business catering to their clients' thirst, hunger, and other inflamed appetites, while those stuck out on the streets simply swelter and mutter curses at the weather.

After six or seven months of continuous heat and humidity, punctuated by occasional thunderstorms and typhoons, the island is bestowed with an annual gift of one or two months of gorgeous, relatively stable weather in October and November. Happily, this is when the most festive national holidays occur and the greatest number of overseas visitors arrive.

Then it turns cold. Like the heat of summer, it is not the *yang* element of temperature but the *yin* factor of humidity that puts the bone-chilling cold in the air of winter. This season can chill the mind as well as the marrow. During winter a few years ago, it started drizzling cold rain in early February and, according to my friends, continued nonstop for forty-five consecutive days. This prolonged bout of dark wet weather left me feeling so cold and depressed that on the twenty-seventh day I packed my bags and flew off to a beach resort in southern India, where I basked in sun and surf until early April, returning just in time for another month of drizzle known as the "Plum Rains." These April showers are an annual event, but they are warm and sporadic rather than cold and constant.

Someone once aptly defined civilization as "the art of communal living." The more crowded a place, the more its inhabitants must stretch their resources and organize themselves into cooperative units, such as family, village, and state. Seen in this light, civilization becomes a matter of necessity, not merely a refined substitute for barbarism.

The Chinese have been living in organized communities and sharing the same land longer than any other people on earth, and therefore, in order to survive and thrive, they have grown more "civilized" than those who enjoy the luxury of boundless space, limitless resources, and sparse population.

Records of Chinese urban life date back almost five thousand years, which gives the Chinese the oldest ongoing civilization on earth and ranks the Chinese people as the world's most experienced city dwellers. One of the first things a visitor discovers in Taiwan, Hong Kong, or any other Chinese community is that the Chinese like crowds and enjoy what other people disdain as "noise." The ever insightful Chinese language describes the crowds and cacaphony of civilized life as *reh-nau,* literally "hot and noisy," a term the Chinese use to denote anything that is fun, exciting, and worthy of attention.

The "teeming millions" of mainland China have already become a cliche, but it is not generally known that Taiwan is even more densely populated than the mainland. The island's twenty million people endure (perhaps "enjoy" would be a better word) a population density of about 540 persons per square kilometer, which makes Taiwan the world's second most crowded place next to Bangladesh. In metropolitan Taipei, where three million of the island's inhabitants live, over ten thousand people share each square kilometer of space. But unlike Bangladesh or the mainland, the people of Taiwan are very well fed and their economy is booming, thanks in part to the traditional Chinese "art of communal living."

Even in the suburbs the Chinese prefer to live in close quarters, stacked in high-rise condominiums rather than spread out in private compounds. The sounds of the neighbor's baby crying, an irate wife loudly berating her husband for some conjugal offense, a television blaring through the window, a dog yapping late into the night — these are all regarded as the

reassuring sounds of human life in its communal state, the "hot and noisy" echos of civilization. How lonely life must be on an American ranch or Swiss chalet, a private yacht or penthouse suite!

In the entire Chinese language there exisits no term for "privacy" in the strictly personal sense of the Western word. The concept has been bred out of the language by five millenia of communal living. The closest equivalent is a term which means both "personal" and "selfish." In other words, the demand for personal privacy in a civilized society is by definition selfish and antithetical to communal life. In a society where everyone knows almost everything about everyone else's business, the Chinese within a family, neighborhood, village, city, or state display remarkable tolerance towards the personal eccentricities of others. Unlike Western societies, where a prominent politician or corporate magnate can be ruined for life by an exposed extramarital affair, unorthodox religious beliefs, or other unconventional behavior, Chinese societies permit their public figures a surprising degree of personal latitude. After all, they're only human.

The lack of personal privacy helps explain the overriding importance of "face" among the Chinese. Face is a traditional Chinese social mechanism used to compensate individuals for lack of privacy. There is little room for personal space in a crowded city — neither physical nor mental — so the Chinese have learned to give face instead. Face helps lubricate the wheels of social intercourse and reduces friction in the inevitably close encounters that mark human relations in the civilized life of big cities. Fictional praise and honorifics are a convenient way to hide unpleasant facts known to all that might otherwise lead to conflict. The Chinese never "rub it in" when they know that someone has suffered a setback at the office or a scandal at home. They'll gossip for hours about it with their friends, but when "face-to-face" with the person in question, they will pretend they know nothing at all about it.

Taipei is the most quintessentially Chinese city in the world today — the modern prodigy of a five-thousand-year-old urban tradition. As the provisional capital of the Republic of China, it exudes that air of self-importance common to all capitals. But unlike some government

capitals, Taipei is also the island's economic and social hub, as well as its cultural center, and this gives the city a frenetic, "hot and noisy" pace of life that can be exhausting to uninitiated visitors, though never boring.

Jangling pedicabs and unpaved streets, shanties and open sewers once gave Taipei a reputation as the "Ugly Duckling" of Asian cities. But since the big building boom that began during the mid-1970s, Taipei has risen like a phoenix from the ashes of its own incinerators to become one of the most dynamic, fast growing, and style-conscious cities of the East. A strange bird of many colored feathers, Taipei's skyline now glitters with soaring skyscrapers that reflect the most modern architecture, while hunkered down below shimmer the glazed tile eaves of traditional Chinese temples. Chic boutiques flaunt the latest fashions from Paris and New York to the electric blare of New Wave music, while right next door a wizened Chinese herbalist grinds ginseng, gypsum, and ox gall on the well-worn wooden counter of a traditional Chinese pharmacy. Chickens squawk and fish flop as buyers and sellers haggle loudly in the city's many open-air markets, but across the street shoppers glide quietly through air-conditioned supermarkets, filling their baskets with cellophaned fruits and precut fillets at fixed prices. Here a family slurps up spicey Szechuan noodles with chopsticks, while their neighbors munch burgers and fries at a fast-food chain down the street. It is all part of a day in the life of Taipei, a chameleon city that, like the climate, defies pat predictions and logical labels.

Taiwan's second largest city and major international seaport, Kaohsiung, lies down along the southern shores of the island. Unabashedly modern and mercantile, Kaohsiung is the motor which powers Taiwan's economic dynamo, while Taipei steers the course. Among its many credits, Kaohsiung is the world's biggest scrapper of old ships. As workers scurry about these huge rusty hulks, blow torches and wrenches in hand, they look like tiny ants busily dismantling the carcass of a giant beetle. Every nut and bolt, winch and wire, is salvaged and sold either as spare parts or nautical artifacts.

Strolling past a nautical antique shop in Kaohsiung a few years ago, a piece of beautifully engraved glass caught my eye. After staring at it through the window for a while, I felt

compelled to go inside for a closer look. Still unable to identify its familiarity, I finally asked the clerk, who replied, "Oh, that piece just arrived from the scrapyards. It came from the bar-room of the *New Amsterdam*." Lo and behold! Ten years earlier I had worked as social director on the *New Amsterdam's* Carribean cruises and had spent many a midnight hour gazing through that engraved glass partition while taking my usual round of nightcaps. It felt strange to find this disembodied fragment of memory hanging forlornly among other relics in a souvenir shop in Taiwan, but on further reflection it seemed no stranger, perhaps even symbolic of, my own presence here.

That's Taiwan — en eclectic blend of East and West, modern and traditional. But do not be fooled by all the glitz and glitter that glows on the surface, especially in Taipei and Kaohsiung. Beneath the modern cosmetics beats a staunchly traditional heart. At a glance, the *yang* of modern influence seems more obvious than the *yin* of traditional culture, but look again and you will find that deep and ancient spring from which the inexhaustible energy of the Chinese people has always flowed. Chinese culture is essentially feminine and aesthetic in nature, not *macho* and aggressive like Japan and the West, and herein lies the secret to the endurance, charm, and vitality of Chinese civilization.

Traditional Chinese culture is the key to the jigsaw of color and contrast in Taiwan. Culture binds the Chinese to their past, makes the present more tolerable, and insulates them from the uncertainties of the future. Culture is also the common denominator in the complex equation of Chinese ethnography, for the Chinese people are as ethnically diverse as the people of Europe. In fact, the word "Chinese" describes a culture, not a race, which means, therefore, that in one sense anyone who embraces that culture can become Chinese.

There are two levels of traditional Chinese culture in Taiwan. The more obvious one is visual and inanimate: priceless art objects on display in museums; traditional arts and crafts in

galleries and shops; temples, monuments, and other classical architecture; elegant calligraphy on everything from sacred altars to advertisements. The more subtle but ultimately more satisfying aspect of Chinese culture in Taiwan is on the human level: the way people live, think, and feel; how they face the world; how they relate to one another.

Chinese culture can be traced to a single source and summed in a single syllable: "Tao." Pronounced "dow" as in Dow Jones, Tao simply means "way" or "path," but its connotations cover "everything under Heaven," from philosophy to physics, martial arts to culinary arts, conjugal relations to international relations. Everything Chinese is rooted in Tao, without whose firm foundation the entire edifice of Chinese civilization would crumble.

The essential principle of the Way is that everything in the universe from the galactic to microscopic level is driven by dynamic tension between two opposite but complementary forces known as *yin* and *yang*. Call them what you will — hot and cold, black and white, positive and negative, fire and water, sun and moon, or, most telling of all, male and female — in the end all phenomena boil down to the eternal cosmic dance of *yin* and *yang*. The key to this way of life is first to recognize the *yin* and the *yang* in a particular process or problem, then balance the two forces in optimum harmony with human conditions. The traditional Western approach to life is to try to resolve contradictions by the conquest of man over nature, right over wrong, the "good guys" over the "bad guys," and other such dualistic dichotomies. The Chinese, however, have been thinking about these problems long enough to realize that truth is not to be found in one side of the equation or the other, but rather in between the two, in the balance of opposites, in the very contradiction itself. This point of view accounts for many elements in Chinese character which foreigners find inscrutable.

The Bible of Taoist philosophy is the beguiling five-thousand word verse known as the *Tao Teh Ching*, or *The Way and Its Power*. Attributed to the Taoist sage Lao-Tze, who lived about 2,500 years ago, the *Tao Teh Ching* ranks as the single most widely translated book in the world today, with over one hundred different translations in print, thirty-eight in English alone. Its appeal, like the culture it engendered, is universal and timeless.

First and foremost, Tao attributes superior power to *yin* over *yang*: "What of all things is most soft/Conquers that which is most hard." Here we find the familiar analogy of water and stone, for everyone knows that water eventually wears the hardest stone to sand. It also refers to the way a woman conquers a man simply by enveloping his hardness in her softness and dousing his fire with her water: "The female by quiescence conquers the male; by quiescence she gets underneath." In a larger context, the "soft" ways of peace are ultimately more potent and lasting than the "hard" ways of war, the pen is mightier than the sword, and the meek shall inherit the earth.

China, with the seductive allure of superior culture, conquered all her conquerors simply by being passive, getting underneath, and absorbing their barbaric hardness with her civilized softness. As a result, China survived while her *macho* aggressors grew weak and finally disappeared entirely from the stage of history. Instead of fighting fire with fire, China fought fire with water and won. Taiwan today wields the same weapon in its ongoing feud with communist rivals on the mainland — the weapon of traditional Chinese culture.

Among the most vivid living reflections of ancient Chinese culture in contemporary Taiwan are the thousands of temples that dot the island. Very little has changed within Chinese temple walls for many centuries, and even the most modern minded people in Taiwan continue to pay frequent homage to their ancient gods. Almost every day of the year on the Chinese calendar marks some traditional festival day, and even Chinese Christian converts occasionally visit traditional temples to keep in touch with native deities, "just in case." Chinese gods are not jealous, and all visitors are equally welcome in their temples, for like the Chinese people, Chinese gods are hospitable and love company.

The traditional Chinese view of life after death is most revealing and explains a lot about how they live on earth. In the Western world, people imagine utopia to be a sort of "heaven on earth," and Western religion attributes superior value to the "kingdom of heaven." But the earthy Chinese imagine the afterlife to be a sort of "earth in heaven," for they regard life on earth to be the best of all possible worlds.

Thanks to the friendly familiarity between heaven and earth, Chinese temples are not the dark, somber, silent houses of worship found in Christian, Jewish, Moslem, and other god-fearing religious traditions. Instead, they are open, airy, cheerful places, where the lively sounds of laughter and conversation mingle with the murmur of prayers and incantations. Old men come to smoke and chat amid the carved columns and exquisitely crafted icons, children romp while their mothers pray for another son, students come to cram for exams in the tranquil courtyards, and on major festival days Chinese temples reverberate with the "heat and noise" of human activity. The carnival atmosphere that often prevails in traditional Chinese temples reflects the Chinese love of life on earth and their hope that the next life will be much the same.

A related reflection of traditional culture in contemporary Taiwan is fortune-telling. As Taiwan reels pell-mell into the high-tech future, this most ancient of Chinese studies has enjoyed a major renaissance at all levels of Chinese society, from corporate tycoons to taxi drivers, movie stars to housewives. As Taipei fortune-teller Newton Wu explains, "Modern life causes so much stress and raises so many problems at home and at work that Chinese people today tend to look for guidance beyond the realm of technology. Western logic and psychology have failed to provide satisfactory answers to the problems of modernization in our traditional society, so people are turning back to the most ancient roots of Chinese philosophy for comfort and advice."

No Chinese contractor in his right mind would dare erect a modern high-rise in Taipei without first consulting a traditional Taoist geomancer to determine the most cosmologically favourable angles for windows, doors, and foundation. Called *feng shui* ("wind and water"), this ancient Chinese science traces the invisible "Dragon Veins" which conduct celestial energies from heaven to earth and thereby locates the most advantageous positions for human dwellings. Prior to elections in Taiwan, some aspiring candidates invite geomancers to their homes and offices to rearrange furniture in such a way that maximum luck — and votes — are attracted to their campaigns. Science or superstition? To the Chinese, this is a moot question.

But if nothing else, such customs at least provide comfort and confidence, which in turn promote success in the tasks at hand.

When it comes to the great transitions of life — birth, marriage, death — the Chinese in Taiwan turn full face to their time-honored traditions, with often exotic results. For example, pregnant women in Taiwan sometimes show up at hospitals several days or weeks prior to term and request immediate delivery by Caesarian section. Why? So that their babies enter this world at precisely the most auspicious hour and day calculated by their astrologers. Since the Year of the Dragon is regarded to be the most favorable time of all to be born in the twelve-year cycle of the Chinese zodiac, the birth rate in Taiwan takes a quantum leap each and every time the Dragon rolls around, requiring the government to build new schools and other facilities to accommodate this cyclical boom of baby dragons. During the other eleven years, modern birth control keeps Taiwan's population growth down to the same low levels current in the West.

Wedding dates, grand openings, contract signings, travel schedules, funerals — all are set according to the arcane science of the Chinese soothsayer and his ancient almanacs. Sceptical Westerners often discount all this as superstition, but the very same Chinese who abide by these ancient ways also excel in the most advanced fields of science and technology.

Indeed, a major reason why the Chinese, like the Koreans and Japanese who learned from them, fare so well in the modern world is precisely because they limit science and technology to the brain and the factory, while continuing to cling to the ancient humanistic ways of their ancestors in matters of the heart and home. They use modern technology to build cars and computers, highways and high-rises, but rely on the time-tested traditions of the past to satisfy the ancient appetites of body and soul. These traditions give them the spiritual strength and self-assurance they need to succeed in this otherwise excessively mechanistic modern world.

Language reflects culture and character more concisely than any other aspect of civilization, especially a language as old and widespread as Chinese, which evolved to its present form about two thousand years ago. If a foreign visitor could suddenly understand the constant din of Chinese chatter heard on the streets of Taipei, he would be surprised, amused, and finally

fascinated by the way the Chinese communicate among themselves.

Listen:

Standing in an elevator on the way to work, Mr Chang turns to his colleague Mr Wu and asks, "*Chir fan-le mei-yo?*" In plain English, what he means is "Hi, how are you?" but in Chinese he actually said, "Have you eaten yet?" In other words, the Chinese assume that what makes a person feel "fine" is the stomach not the mind and that food is the source of one's mood. Among Chinese, the way to a man's heart runs through his stomach.

After work that evening, Mr. Chang and Mr. Wu go out for drinks and dinner, and the discussion turns to family matters. Mr. Chang, who keeps a mistress, explains to his friend, "House plants are not as fragrant as wild flowers." His friend nods in acknowledgement of this ancient wisdom, but points out, "Be careful — wild blossoms have thorns!" Meanwhile back home, Mr. Chang's wife, who knows all about her husband's philandering, shrugs it all off with a knowing remark about men, "All crows under Heaven are the same color black!"

How does a language whose written symbols haven't changed for two millenia deal with the terms of modern science and the concerns of contemporary society? Here's how: in Chinese electricity is "lightning" and thus a computer is a "lightning brain" and a telegram is a "lightning report." An airplane is a "flying machine," cement is "water and mud," chemistry is "the study of transformation," and psychology is "the study of heart patterns."

The literal meanings of many contemporary Chinese terms can jolt you back to ancient times. Among my favorites are the words for contradiction (literally "spear and shield"), landscape ("mountains and water"), quickly ("by horse"), corn ("jade rice"), rocket ("fire arrow"), and faucet ("water dragon head"). When you speak Chinese, you automatically clothe even the most modern ideas in the costume of ancient images, and the constant use of classical allusions in Chinese keeps the past alive. Small wonder the Chinese never seem to suffer from "future shock": they paint the future in the familiar images of ancient times.

*R*en-ching-wei — the flavor of human feeling — has always been the hallmark of Chinese society, and it remains the essential human distillate of traditional Chinese culture in Taiwan. For those who focus on people instead of places, inner character rather than outer appearances, this human flavor is strongly evident in Taiwan and usually leaves a pleasant after-taste.

To describe human feelings in terms of flavor is typical of the sensory-oriented Chinese. Adjectives such as sweet and sour, bitter and pungent, crop up frequently in Taiwan when conversation turns to human relations and personal character. The full spectrum of human emotions is reflected in Chinese *ren-ching-wei* — joy and sorrow, anger and fear, laughter and tears — and all come into play in a typical day in the life of the Chinese in Taiwan.

Foreigners are often surprised, occasionally embarassed, by the emotional exuberance of the Chinese, who like to give vent to strong feelings. The streets and markets of Taipei ring with laughter, wrangling, greetings, and colorful curses, but the Chinese take very little of this literally. Instead, the point is this: when your heart is full of feeling — sweet, sour, bitter, or whatever the "flavor" may be — open up and let the steam out, then proceed with the business at hand. Thanks to this social mechanism of emotional expression, life among the Chinese in Taiwan is refreshingly free of the stress and neurosis that cramp human happiness in more emotionally inhibited societies.

A basic social tenet of *ren-ching-wei* is that family and friends always come first, business and politics second. In a survey conducted in Taipei in 1984, residents from all walks of life were asked to list the following items in order of importance in their lives: wealth, love, social life, work, politics, and family. The overwhelming majority listed family first, followed in order of preference by work, love, and wealth. Politics earned a distant last place on the list of Chinese priorities.

Due to the focus on family and friends in Chinese society, the Chinese naturally prefer to do business with relatives and well established acquaintances rather than strangers, a practice scorned in the legalistic West as cronyism and nepotism. Yet the Chinese way not only makes

good human sense, it also made good business sense. All other factors being equal, you can usually trust a friend or relative more than you can a stranger, and even if, despite the bonds of family or friendship, a contract is broken or a check bounces, you have far more leverage and practical recourse if the scoundrel is tied into your private network of personal connections, or *guan-hsi*, than if he were a stranger.

Personal *guan-hsi* among the Chinese are constantly renewed by the ritual exchange of gifts and favors. Every gift or favor granted fattens the donor's credit account with the recipients of his largesse, who are obliged by the rules of the game to repay in kind some day.

These rules are far more binding and hence more effective than any rules of law, because to betray them would immediately send shudders of doubt and scorn reverberating throughout one's entire *guan-hsi* network. Betraying friends or family is a far more heinous offense in Chinese society than breaking the law. For the Chinese, a public court of law is always the very last resort for settling personal disputes. It is also a clear indication that the plaintif has insufficient personal connections to settle his own private problems himself, and consequently judges often rule against the plaintif, even if he is technically right, because by dragging his personal affairs into a public court rather than settling them privately through personal *guan-hsi* he has already committed a philosophical, if not legal, mistake.

The over-riding importance of family, friends, and other personal relations inevitably has a negative impact on the public domain. Sun Yat-sen, the founding father of the Republic of China, who spent years trying to rally the Chinese people behind his nationalist cause during the early decades of the twentieth century, lamented, "The Chinese have familyism and clanism, but they don't have nationalism." This lack of public concern is reflected, for example, in the rude driving habits that prevail throughout Taiwan, in the pernicious pollution of the environment, in the shoving and elbowing for position that occurs whenever people line up at bus and train stations, movie theatres, post offices, and other public facilities.

Such apathy towards the public domain reflects neither malice nor ignorance. Instead, it reflects the very pragmatic Chinese view that everyone in the public domain is, by definition, a

stranger and therefore does not deserve the same respect and courtesy accorded to family, friends, colleagues, and others with whom one has close personal ties. That's why those who make personal friends in Taiwan inevitably have a good time here, and businessmen who learn to rely on private rather than public channels usually get a lot more done.

One of the most succinct expressions of the flavor of human feeling that lies at the heart of traditional Chinese philosophy and lifestyle is the very first line Confucius chose to open his classic masterpiece *Lun Yü*, known in English translation as *The Analects of Confucius*. This book, which had to be memorized by all aspiring scholars and statesmen in old China, opens with the heart-warming line, "When friends visit from afar, is this not indeed a pleasure!" Thus the Great Sage of Chinese civilization clearly states that the first and foremost pleasure of civilized life is friendship, which in turn affords the opportunity to practice the greatest of all civilized arts — human hospitality.

When friends visit, they must be fed and sheltered, entertained and honored. It doesn't matter whether they come from next door or the next village, a distant city or halfway around the world, it is their act of visiting which affords the host his pleasure. By offering them the best food and drink at his disposal and catering to their every need, the host shows what great pleasure he takes in their friendship and further re-enforces their links of *guan-hsi*. This attitude accounts for the abiding importance of hospitality in Chinese society, especially the grand social tradition known as *ching-keh*, "inviting guests."

People caught in the clutches of excessively cerebral concerns will benefit greatly by lingering for a while among the Chinese people in Taiwan. The human heat and noise and unbridled sensual indulgence that prevail in night markets and other nocturnal haunts in Taiwan provide precisely the prescription required to soothe the febrile churnings of the overworked brain and focus attention instead on the senses, the stomach, and other organs of instant gratification. The Chinese work very hard by day, perhaps harder than anyone else, but they always balance the bitterness of work with the sweetness of pleasure, compensate for the labors of day with the delights of night, and pay equal heed to the needs of body and brain.

This balanced perspective on human nature is one reason why traditional Chinese societies such as Taiwan are relatively free of the neuroses and psychoses, stress and strain, violent crime and other social pathology that other contemporary societies have come to take for granted as inevitable consequences of modern life in the industrial age. But it is neither modern times nor life itself that is responsible for all the human misery suffered in so many "advanced" industrial societies. It is ignorance of human nature and arrogance towards Mother Nature that are to blame, and this is one subject in which the whole world could stand to learn some valuable lessons from the flourishing traditional society of the Chinese in Taiwan, where people not only thoroughly enjoy life but also perform remarkably well in the modern arts of science and technology, industry and trade.

To foreign eyes, this way of life may seem merely quaint, perhaps even contrived, but to the Chinese it's the only way to live. With five millenia of experience in the art of communal living behind them, the Chinese in Taiwan today don't worry too much about the future. The Chinese view history as cyclical rather than linear, which means that the past reflects whatever the future might hold. Indeed, the Chinese view of time lies at the very heart of the Chinese way of life.

The Chinese word for "future" is based on an ideogram that means "behind" or "in back of," unlike Western thought, which sees the future as lying "before" us. In fact, however, the future is a blank that no one can predict, much less see, and so the Chinese notion that the future lies unseen "behind" us while the past is an open book that lies "before" us is essentially correct.

On the other hand, the Chinese refer to the past with a word that also means "in front of," and it is to the past that the Chinese turn their eyes to look for reflections of the future. Since "time and tide for no man wait," it doesn't really matter whether you face the future like the West or face the past like the Chinese, for time marches on relentlessly. But in the mean time, the Chinese view reveals the rich tapestry of a long and colorful history, along with all the lessons it holds for the present.

As the Chinese in Taiwan gaze out across the Taiwan Straits and look at what's happening on the mainland today, they see a situation there very similar to conditions that prevailed over 2,000 years ago. When the militant Kingdom of Chin (from whom the West derived the word "China") swept down from the northwest in 221 BC, they united the entire country under the harsh rule of the emperor Chin Shih-huang, who burned the Confucian classics, buried dissident scholars alive, and enslaved millions of his subjects to toil their lives away building the Great Wall of China.

True, he imposed order on China at a time of chaos, and he gave China the discipline it needed to take a giant historical step forward as a unified state under a single central government, effectively ending two millenia of feudalism in only two decades. But he rode rough-shod over the niceties of Chinese civilization and repeatedly violated China's ancient humanistic traditions. Tired of his brutal reign, the Chinese people shrugged off his legacy of terror within a single generation and steered the country back onto the well worn grooves traveled by their ancestors. This cultural revival occured during the great Han Dynasty, which enshrined Confucius as the national sage and set the pattern for a dozen dynasties to follow. It is from the Han that the Chinese adopted the name that they still use in reference to themselves today—*han-ren*—"People of Han."

Han Chinese civilization continues to thrive in contemporary Taiwan, reflected everywhere in images old and new, and if the Chinese are right about their own history, then it's only a matter of time before the ever shifting winds of history blow the spores of traditional Chinese culture back to where they once belonged.

PREVIOUS PAGES: A field of catkins blooming in the dawn along Taiwan's scenic east coast. The island's flora reflects a lush blend of tropical and alpine elements, especially in the rugged central mountains and along the craggy coastal cliffs of the eastern seaboard. Taiwan's abundant vegetation is one reason why early Chinese settlers, accustomed to the drought and famine of the mainland, called it "Treasure Island."

A panoramic view of Sun Moon Lake and surrounding hills in central Taiwan, is seen from the top tier of the towering Pagoda of Filial Piety. Sun Moon Lake was one of former President Chiang Kai-shek's favorite retreats in Taiwan, and he sponsored construction of many classical sights there.

LEFT AND ABOVE: Dense foliage envelopes the wooded trail that leads to the Dragon Valley Waterfall in Ku Kuan, the first hill station on the scenic East-West Cross-Island Highway, known more popularly as "The Rainbow of Treasure Island." This serpentine mountain road winds its way for 120 km through the Central Range, connecting the western plains with the eastern seaboard.

後頁：破曉時分，沿着景色挺秀的台灣東海岸怒放的柔荑花田。

自慈恩塔頂層可眺望日月潭與羣山環繞的全景。日月潭是台灣最受遊客喜愛的蜜月勝地。

左，上：濃鬱的叢林遮蔽了通往谷關龍谷瀑布的林蔭小徑。谷關是有「寶島彩虹」之稱的東西橫貫公路的第一座山站。

LEFT: The cliff-hugging boardwalk along the boulder strewn Foggy River in Taroko Gorge, east Taiwan. This marvelous marble canyon is the island's most famous natural wonder and draws 5,000 visitors daily. "Taroko" means "beautiful" in the dialect of the aboriginal Ami tribe, who inhabit this region.

ABOVE: A bridge and staircase traverse river and boulders to give access to a classical Chinese pavilion perched on a mossy promontory in Taroko Gorge. The guardian lion in the foreground is crafted of pure marble at the coastal town of Hualien, from raw marble mined in the mountains of Taroko Gorge.

左：懸崖憑欄，下望東台灣太魯閣滿佈圓石的立霧溪峽谷。「太魯閣」在台灣山胞阿眉族語言中是「美麗」的意思。

上：橫跨湍流、峽谷的橋樑與階徑導引遊客登上太魯閣屹立於綠苔巖峯上的長春亭。前方的石獅子是花蓮特產純大理石雕造的。

Sculpted into bizarre shapes by centuries of wind and waves, the stone figures of Yeh Liu ("Wild Willows") stare out to sea along Taiwan's northern coastline. At right is the famous "Queen's Head," whose profile bears a striking resemblence to ancient Egypt's Queen Nefertiti. The Chinese have always expressed profound appreciation for natural works of art produced by nature's elements— water worn stones, wind swept shores, oddly shaped trees, waterfalls, sunsets, and misty mountains.

OVERLEAF: Fertile farmlands fill the plains en route to Sun Moon Lake in central Taiwan. Arguably the world's most efficient farmers, the Chinese have been tilling the earth for over 5,000 years. As ancient agriculturists, the Chinese could hardly believe their eyes when they discovered fecund, forested and abundantly watered "Treasure Island" floating only a short sail off the frequently famined coast of mainland China.

台灣北海岸野柳飽經數世紀風吹浪打塑造出來的怪石。右圖像極了古埃及皇后的頭部雕像。

前頁：往台灣中部日月潭的途中，平原上四處可見豐饒的農田。這些繁榮的農田也使得台灣居民成為自日本到以色列之間亞洲吃得最好的人們。

At 60,000 strong, the Amis are Taiwan's largest aboriginal tribe. While other aborigines like to hunt and fish for a living, the Amis prefer agriculture. Their ancient week-long Harvest Festival, held in Hualien in August, is one of the most colorful extravaganzas in the Far East. The Amis are renowned as great singers and dancers and Wen Mei-kui, known as the Ami "Empress of Mountain Song," performed at the White House for President Reagan.

台灣東部花蓮的阿眉族山地女郎在鏡頭前笑嫣盛綻。每年八月在花蓮舉行為期一週的傳統阿眉族豐年祭，十彩繽紛，是遠東最富盛名的民俗盛典。

The 2,500-year-old "Book of Odes," compiled by Confucius, contains numerous poems describing happy farmers laughing and joking, flirting and courting, as they tend their fields. These farms along the east coast are timelessly Chinese and reflect the historical fact that Taiwan's highly refined urban culture has always been supported by a solid backbone of agriculture.

台灣東海岸的農家樂不僅是典型的中國畫面，也反映了農業始終是都市精緻文化最大支柱的歷史事實。

Ancient patterns still prevail in Taiwan's agricultural sector, despite high-tech lifestyles in the cities. An ox-drawn wagon carries a farmer and his wife out to the fields north of Tainan, while a water buffalo pulls a traditionally crafted plow through a rice paddy near Fengkang. The gentle, good natured water buffalo is the most endearing of all Chinese domestic animals and has become an enduring symbol of tradition in Taiwan.

台灣北部農村中一對夫婦趕着牛車去工作；而在南部楓港，一隻水牛正在犂田。

Early birds stretch their "wings" for flight at the Chiang kai-shek Memorial park in Taipei, while two little "fledglings" look on from the sidelines. All over Taiwan you will see such groups gathering at dawn in parks and gardens, along lakes and rivers, to prepare body and mind for another day of work and play with traditional Chinese calisthenics, breathing exercises, and other "Long Life" regimens.

台北早起的人們在中正紀念堂前作晨操，一旁的兩隻「幼虎」捉狹又觀望。

ABOVE: The classical entrance to the ornate temple called "Palace of Martial and Literary Arts" in Kaohsiung is flanked by the modern urban clutter of cars and plastic shop signs. Such contrasts between past and present, traditional and contemporary, are common sights throughout Taiwan, but to the Chinese, steeped as they are in the subtle philosophy of Yin and Yang, such contrasts present no contradiction.

RIGHT: A policewoman in a stylist hat and "go-go" boots supervises traffic at a busy intersection in downtown Taipei. A random sampling of signs in the background read, "Beef Noodles," "Treasure Island Optical Co.," "Celestial Dragon Portraits," and "Northwest Hotel." In former times, shop signs such as these were painted onto long banners and hung from the eaves of storefronts.

上：夾在鬧區車輛與商店招牌之間的高雄文武宮正門，這正是台灣普遍可見的過去與現在、傳統與當代的對比。

右：頭戴歐式新穎的帽子，足登流行短靴，女警察正在台北市區十字路口指揮交通。

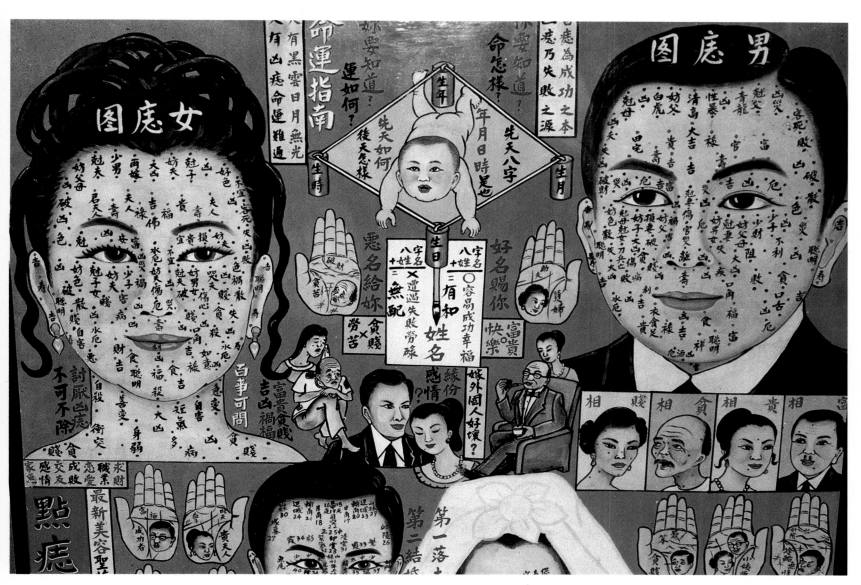

LEFT: Pop art posters advertise foreign films in Taipei's bustling West Gate district, the city's own version of New York's Times Square. Since 1949, the Chinese in insular Taiwan have consistently posted one of the world's highest per capita consumption rates for movies, but since the lifting of restrictions on outbound travel in 1978, more and more people are opting to roam abroad and see the world in person, rather than through the rose-colored lenses of Hollywood.

ABOVE: This is not an advertisement for a facial blemish cream, but rather a poster marking the shop of a face-reading fortune teller in Taipei. Each point on the face reflects a specific character trait. In recent years, traditional Chinese fortune telling has made a big comeback in Taiwan, as people harried and hurried by modern lifestyles, search for security and comfort in the occult arts of their ancestors.

左：有如紐約時報廣場的台北西門町電影街，人潮洶湧。外國影片的廣告看板傾向普普藝術風格。

上：這不是潤膚面霜廣告，是相面館掛的男女痣圖。最近幾年，傳統中國算命重又盛行起來。

LEFT: The hourly changing of the guard at the National Revolutionary Martyr's Shrine in Taipei. This building is one of the city's most faithful reflections of classical Chinese architecture in the imperial palace style of the Forbidden City in Peking. The shrine is dedicated to the memory of war heroes who died in the struggle to establish and defend the Republic of China.

ABOVE: An honor guard stands sentry at the entrance to the National Revolutionary Martyr's Shrine. Taiwan's armed forces rank among the best trained and best equipped in East Asia, and they stand determined to defend the island against their implacable foes across the Taiwan Straits.

左：在台北最具北京皇宮建築風味的忠烈祠前，儀隊每小時換崗一次。

上：台北忠烈祠站崗的儀隊。台灣的三軍是東亞訓練與裝備並列最優的軍力。

LEFT: The Chiang Kai-shek Memorial sparkles under floodlights on the evening of Double Ten Day (October 10), which marks the founding of the Republic of China in 1911. This massive memorial reflects the same style of classical architecture used for the Sun Yat-sen Memorial in Nanking on the mainland. The entrance gate was aligned and positioned according to the ancient principles of *feng-shui* (geomancy), to insure optimum exposure to celestial energy coursing through cosmic "Dragon Veins" in the vicinity.

ABOVE: The Presidential Palace festooned with lights, banners, bunting, and auspicious slogans for the annual Double Ten Day parade in Taipei. This building was constructed by the Japanese during their half century occupation of Taiwan and reflects the eccentric blend of Edwardian English and traditional Oriental styles favored by early 20th-century Japan.

OVERLEAF: The intersection of Lin Sen North Road and Min Chuan East Road in Taipei, a city that looks her best by the neon light of night. As the world's most experienced and enthusiastic city dwellers, the Chinese have naturally cultivated a rich and highly refined tradition of nightlife. As one sybaritic visitor remarked, "In Taipei, every night seems to be Saturday night!"

左：雙十國慶夜晚燈火如畫中的台北中正紀念堂。此一宏偉建築與大陸南京的中山陵屬於同一風格。

上：爲迎接每年一度的國慶盛大遊行，總統府與四近燈火通明，國旗飄揚，張燈結綵，端的是「光輝的十月」。

前頁：台北市林森北路與民權東路交叉口。可以看出霓虹燈下的台北市夜色尤其迷人。有些外籍遊客覺得：「在台北，似乎每天晚上都像週末。」

Chinese women practice a popular local form of aerobic dancing in a public park in Taichung. A blend of ballroom dancing, deep breathing, and Chinese grace, this healthy regimen is a uniquely feminine manifestation of the traditional Chinese penchant for starting the day with an invigorating round of early morning exercise.

OVERLEAF: As bride and groom pose for the camera in a wedding photography studio in Taipei. Formal western wedding attire has become *de rigueur* in Taiwan, although wedding rites and wedding banquets remain staunchly traditional. Like western Europe and America, young Chinese in Taiwan are now getting married later in life, having fewer children, and are less reluctant to dissolve unhappy unions by divorce.

台中市公園內，一羣婦女正在練韻律舞蹈。

前頁：新婚夫婦在照相館中拍結婚照片。台灣年輕人結婚雖然都穿西式禮服，婚禮與喜宴却仍依循傳統的習俗。與西方一樣，台灣的年輕人也流行晚婚，少生孩子也比較不怕離婚了。

ABOVE: A craftsman in Lukang uses the traditional tools of his trade to mount Chinese paintings on wall scrolls. Classical Chinese calligraphy and painting remain a living tradition in Taiwan, and almost every home on the island displays at least one or two excellent samples on its walls.

RIGHT: Master calligrapher Mr. Liu Cheng-hu demonstrates his delicate art in his studio in Peitou, north of Taipei. The ideogram he has just brushed onto paper is *jing,* which means "tranquility." Since ancient times, Chinese scholars have cultivated the art of calligraphy, using the "Four Treasures of the Scholar's Studio," all of which appear in this picture: brush, paper, ink, and inkstone. To the practiced Chinese eye, a man's calligraphy "reflects his soul like a mirror."

上：鹿港的傳統裱糊師傅正用傳統工器裱糊中國畫。

右：書法家劉正鵠在他台北近郊北投的畫室中大筆揮毫。

Lukang, or "Deer Harbor," located along Taiwan's west coast, was the original port of entry for waves of Chinese immigrants from the mainland during the big exodus of the 17th century. Now silted up, the harbor is closed, but the town itself remains one of the most authentic enclaves of traditional Chinese arts and crafts on the island. Almost all of Taiwan's major temples have their altars, icons, statues, and other accessories hand crafted in Lukang. At left, a shopkeeper takes a long-distance order amid the clutter of temple arts on display in his shop. At right, a craftswoman carefully paints the finishing touches onto a wooden icon carved by another craftsman, as her apprentice son studiously looks on.

座落於台灣西海岸的鹿港，是十七世紀大陸移民浪潮在台灣上岸的最早港口。幾乎台灣所有廟宇神像與擺設均出自鹿港藝師之手。在圖中店主正以長途電話與客戶談生意。右圖，女畫師正為別人雕刻的神像着色，她的兒子一旁專心學習。

ABOVE: A lukang vendor ties a bundle of paper "money" for sale to a customer prior to a major festival. Money, cars, baots, houses, and other objects of value made of scented paper are burned as symbolic offerings to deities and spirits of deceased ancestors.

RIGHT: A clerk tallies up a bill on the ancient Chinese abacus in a tea shop in Lukang. Taiwan produces some of the world's best Chinese teas, and confirmed connoisseurs pay up to US$50 per ounce for rare vintage blends plucked by hand from remote plantations in the misty mountains of the Central Range.

上：鹿港店販在節慶拜拜之前將紙錢綑好，準備大發利市。

右：鹿港茶葉舖中，掌櫃的仍用算盤。台灣茶葉品質馳名全球。特等茶葉售價高達美金五十元一兩。

The Constant Cure: Chinese herbalists have been dispensing healing remedies culled from nature ever since the dawn of history. Top, a Taipei pharmacist weighs Chinese Wolfberry for a herbal prescription presented by a patient. Above, a woman sorts tea leaves next door. Tea itself is regarded as a therapeutic herb with potent medicinal properties.

台北一家中藥舖中，藥師按方爲病人配藥。下圖是隔隣一家茶葉店的老太太正在篩選茶葉。茶葉本身也具中藥的功能。

Above are the basic tools of the herbalist's trade: dried herbs, mortar and pestle for pounding, paper for wrapping, and an abacus for calculating. Over 2,000 medicinal herbs are listed in the Chinese pharmocopeia.

OVERLEAF: A traditional physician in Taipei jokes with a patient as he adjusts acupuncture needles in her legs. From the points he has needled, the patient probably suffers from a digestive disorder. Acupuncture, which is becoming an increasingly popular therapy throughout the world, promotes healing and accelerates recovery by manipulating the body's vital energy through an invisible but powerful network of energy channels called "meridiens." Despite the needles, the therapy is virtually painless.

中國草藥用加蓋的陶瓷罐子或分隔的小木箱裝存，如上圖。下圖中展示的是中藥店中不可少的器材。

前頁：台北一位中醫師爲病人針灸時，兩人有說有笑，病人顯然並無「針扎之痛」。針灸治療目前在全球各地已普遍流行。

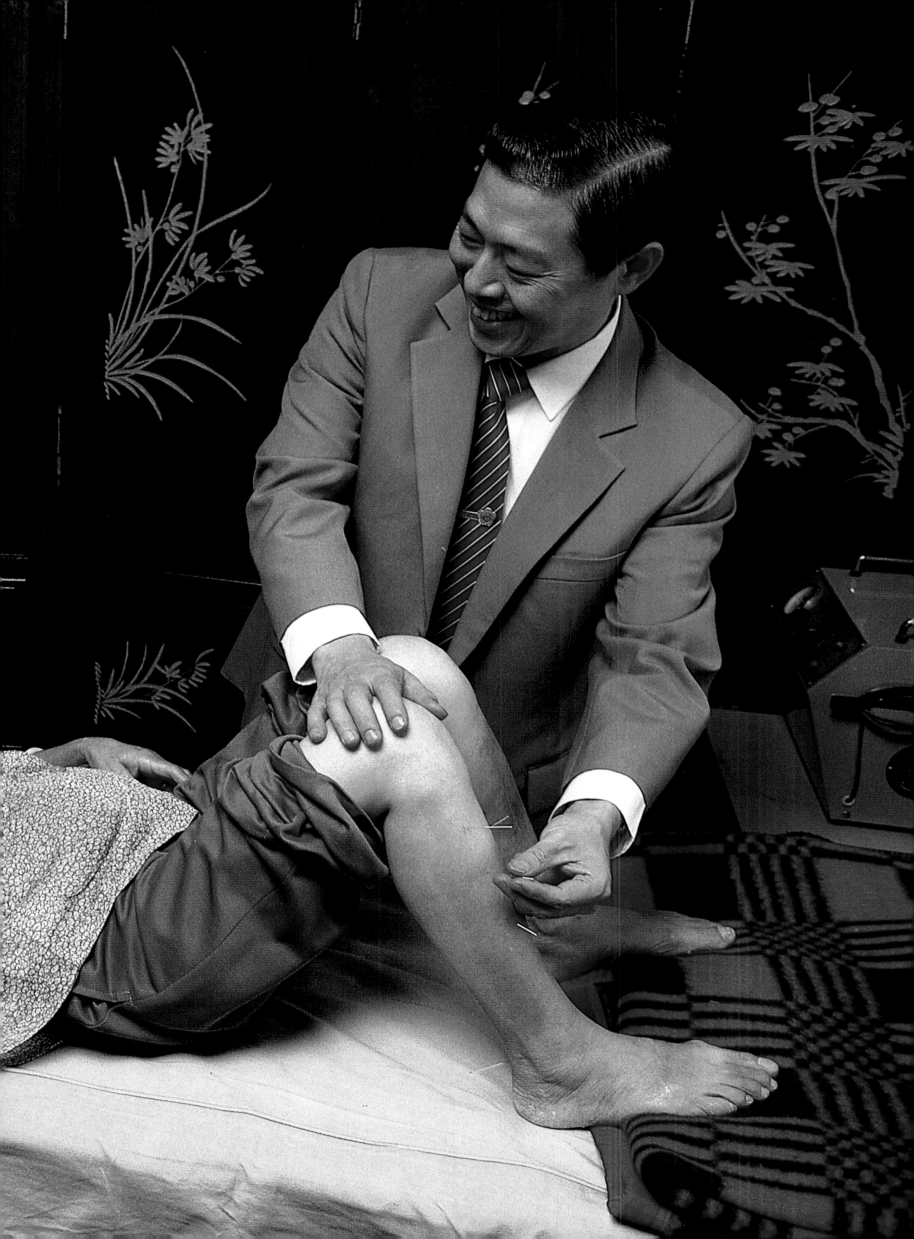

LEFT: A huge statue of Buddha surrounded by dozens of smaller life-size sculptures stands serenely over the entrance to the "Light of Buddha Mountain" in southern Taiwan. This retreat was established by a mendicant monk who attracted an enormous following in Taiwan, and has since become one of the most important centers of Buddhist studies in the Far East.

ABOVE: A visitor at the Light of Buddha Mountain imitates the mudra (hand gesture) displayed by Buddhist statuary there. Mudras are symbolic gestures which when performed together with mantras (chants) and deep meditation have powerful spiritual benefits. The mudra shown here is called "Dispelling Fear" and is used to calm frightened souls and dispel fearsome spirits.

左：台灣南部佛教勝地佛光山入口處，一尊巨佛矗立於數十尊小佛之上。

上：佛光山拜佛的信徒模仿佛像，作出「驅邪」的手勢。

ABOVE: Vermilion lacquered columns support the long colonnades which connect the various shrine halls, temples, and altar rooms at Light of Buddha Mountain. In Taiwan, visiting temples is usually a family affair, and the ambiance is always light and cheery.

RIGHT: A woman and her children pray at the altar of Ma Tsu, Goddess of the Sea and one of Taiwan's most beloved patron deities, at the Ma Tsu temple in Peikang, central Taiwan. The rapid modernization of Taiwan has not eroded traditional Chinese religious life. In fact, the pressures of modern times have made the Chinese more devoted than ever to their ancient pantheon of protective deities.

上：朱紅漆釉的圓柱支撐了連結佛光山大小寺院與神殿的幽長柱廊。

右：台灣中部北港媽祖廟內，媽媽帶着孩子祭拜台灣人最崇拜的媽祖神。

LEFT: An elderly devotee in Lukang strikes a note on the "Wooden Fish," a traditional Chinese temple instrument that makes a deeply resonant "thonk" when struck. It is designed to attract the attention of the temple's resident deities and to dispell idle thought from the mind of the devotee. In the background stands a pyramid of miniature shrines, each of which is dedicated to the spirit of a deceased benefactor of the temple.

ABOVE: Offerings of incense, paper money, and other ritual objects transformed into pure essence by the flames of an ancient censer in a temple in Lukang. The flames consume the objects' 'gross" material form and send the essence curling up to Heaven in smoke. Hence, such offerings are called "smoke prayers."

左：鹿港一位年邁的信徒敲着木魚誦經。她身後堆列整齊的牌位表彰了每一個生前對該廟有貢獻的信徒。

上：香、紙錢與其他祭品，在鹿港一座廟宇的古老香爐的火焰中都化作了虔淨的輕烟。

ABOVE: A bronze censer at the Lung Shan Temple in Taipei constantly ablaze with incense and other offerings. The figure depicted here—with top hat, curly beard, and breeches—probably reflects early Chinese contacts with European traders during the 17th century, when this temple was founded.

RIGHT: A Taoist shaman in trance invokes a protective deity during a temple seance in southern Taiwan. Capped in elaborate head-gear, he flails a bullwhip and a pennant as he communes with the world of spirits. Taoist shamans in Taiwan are often contracted by grieving families to communicate with the spirits of recently deceased relatives.

上：台北龍山寺內的青銅香爐終年香火不斷。火焰前頭的塑像或許追溯着十七世紀這座廟宇興建之初中國人與歐洲人之間的貿易往來。

右：南台灣一座廟宇中，一名道士正聚精滙神地作法請神。

LEFT: A woman temple attendant recites sutras at the Hsing Tien Temple in Taipei, the city's most popular house of worship. Every sacred syllable uttered within the walls of a temple earns merit for the supplicant's soul and helps insure a favorable rebirth in the next life.

ABOVE: There are no generation gaps in the Chinese temples of Taiwan. At the Lung Shan Temple in Taipei, an old granny and a stylish young woman pray to the same traditional gods that have sustained the Chinese soul for thousands of years. The Chinese utilize modern science and technology as practical tools for social and economic progress, but they stick to the traditions of their ancestors in spiritual matters.

左：在台北香火最盛的廟宇行天宮內，一名長年守廟的老婦人正在誦經。

上：在台灣的寺廟中，是沒有代溝的。台北龍山寺內，一位老婆婆與一名穿著入時的少婦膜拜的是同樣的神明。

PREVIOUS PAGE: Women attendants kneel in prayer at Taipei's Hsing Tien Temple, located at the intersection of Min Chuan East Rd and Sung Kiang Rd. These blue-robed women enter the service of the temple as a sort of psychotherapy for neurosis, depression, stress, and other common mental or emotional afflictions. The therapy is remarkably effective, for most of these women fully recover their equilibrium and usually opt to remain in the service of the temple to express their gratitude. Buddhism, which has often been called a "science of mind," seems to understand and deal with the human psyche much better than modern analytical psychology, which perhaps accounts for Buddhism's enduring popularity and continuing growth throughout the world.

LEFT: A future ballet star flexes her legs at the Crown Dance Workshop in Taipei. The gragarious Chinese have always been very adept at the performing arts, and today ballet and modern dance are cultivated side by side with traditional performing arts such as Chinese opera, puppet theater, acrobatics, and classical Chinese music.

ABOVE: Three aspiring ballerinas practice at the bar. Training is very rigorous among Chinese performing artists, who take their art as seriously as traditional painters and calligraphers. In old China, performing artists had a very low social standing, but in Taiwan today they often achieve "superstar" status.

後頁：座落於台北市民權東路與松江路口的行天宮內，婦女信徒跪列祈禱。她們服務性地長年誦經，也是一種祈求內心安寧的心理治療。

左：台北皇冠舞蹈工作室中，「明日芭蕾之星」正在苦練。

上：今天在台灣，一名成功的舞者已可以享有極高的聲譽了。這三名小舞者練起舞來可也是一本正經的。

LEFT: A dancer from the Cloud Gate troupe in Taipei takes a break during rehearsal. Cloud Gate has established a worldwide reputation for its daringly innovative modern dance renditions of traditional Chinese themes.

ABOVE: A lithe dancer struts her stuff during a rehearsal of the Cloud Gate troupe in Taipei. Chinese physique seems to be very well suited for classical Western ballet as well as modern dance, and Cloud Gate has pioneered the fusion of Western forms with Eastern themes.

左：台北雲門舞集中的一名舞者練舞之後小憩片刻。雲門舞集以「傳統中求創新」的風格享譽國際。

上：線條柔婉的雲門舞集舞者或許証實了中國人的身材其實蠻適合跳西方古典芭蕾與現代舞的。

PREVIOUS PAGE: Modern choreography used to tell a traditional story at a performance by the Department of Dance at the National Institute of Arts in Taipei. Many Chinese dancers keep in shape for the stage by practicing traditional martial arts.

ABOVE: The National Institute of Arts' Department of Dance performs a piece entitled "Ami Harvest Festival." Aborigine themes are becoming increasingly popular in all the arts in Taiwan, including music, dance, painting, and sculpture.

RIGHT: A tribal procession in the National Institute of Arts' rendition of "Ami Harvest Festival." Taiwan's aborigine tribes are particularly noted for their colorful costumes, their love of song and dance, and their robust, earthy character. To the highly refined Chinese soul, they satisfy a deep primal craving for an occasional taste of the primitive.

後頁：台北國立藝術學院舞蹈系學生的演出，以現代的編舞意念詮譯了傳統的主題。

上：國立藝術學院舞蹈系演出山地舞「阿眉族豐年祭」。

右：國立藝術學院演出的「阿眉族豐年祭」最能表現阿眉族服飾艷麗、能歌善舞與豪邁健康的特性。

Student actresses prepare for a performance of traditional Chinese opera, also
known as "Peking Opera," at the
National Fuhsing Opera School. Much
of the story in Chinese opera is symboli-
cally told by face paint and costumes,
both of which are very colorful, ornate,
and complex. At left, an actress tries to
jam her foot into a bootie made for the
"Three Inch Golden Lilly," as bound
feet were called in old China.

國立復興戲劇學校的學生演員正在化
裝，準備演出京戲。左圖，一名女演
員在綁蹻，以期能在台上「蓮步生姿」。

LEFT: A Chinese opera actor in full face paint and elaborate head gear glares at the camera prior to his performance on stage at the National Armed Forces Cultural Activities Center in Taipei. Originally, actors wore painted masks,, which were awkward and muffled their voices, but about 1,200 years ago, they started painting the "masks" directly onto their faces.

ABOVE LEFT AND ABOVE: Scenes from a traditional Chinese opera performance at the National Fuhsing Opera School, one of the world's few authentic training grounds for this ancient art.

左：台北國軍文藝活動中心後台，一名裝扮好的淨角凝視鏡頭。

上左，上：國立復興戲劇學校演出京劇一景。這樣道地訓練傳統京劇人才的學校，在今天已經所餘無幾了。

One of the most popular forms of traditional entertainment in Taiwan is "street opera," a local offshoot of Peking Opera performed on make shift stages in open-air markets and side-streets. Formerly, all roles – including female – were played by men, but today tables have turned and women often play the roles of vigorous male heroes, such as the one pictured at the right.

台灣最受廣大民衆喜愛的傳統娛樂，是常露天演出的歌仔戲。以往歌仔戲全由男性演出，如今則完全是女演員的天下了，右圖就是一個例証。

LEFT: An elaborate set for a musical variety show at the China Television Station in Taipei. Television has become the major focus of popular entertainment in Taiwan, and most of the shows are Chinese versions of popular American formulas: heart-throbbing soap operas; cheery TV quiz shows; extravagant variety shows; and slick news broadcasts.

ABOVE: Gyrating chorus dancers have become a "must" on all television variety shows in Taiwan. Here a popular rock singer belts out a tune as rose-haired dancers provide go-go counterpoint. Teenagers in Taipei are beginning to imitate the hair styles and clothing of TV pop stars, much to the dismay of their parents.

左：台北華視電視頻道一項綜藝節目的錄製場面。電視是台灣大衆娛樂的焦點。

上：由於青少年的風靡，台灣電視綜藝節目中的演唱幾乎都有裝扮與動作極爲「新潮」的配舞。

ABOVE: Co-hosts of one of Taiwan's most successful variety shows exchange a round of jokes. The robust lady is known as "The Fat Beauty," and her meek partner falls frequent prey to her predatory remarks and pranks, in a kind of local Chinese version of Laurel and Hardy.

RIGHT: Teen throb rock star, complete with dark glasses and neck-length locks á la Michael Jackson, wails a tune into the microphone at the China Television Station.

上：華視收視率頗高的綜藝節目「雙星報喜」的主持人之一鄒美儀素有「胖美人」之稱，深受觀眾喜愛。

右：出現在華視節目中的「青春偶像」級的歌星。十年之前，像他這副長髮披肩、掛墨鏡的打扮還不一定上得了電視呢。

An historical drama about China's most famous *femme fatale*— a sort of Chinese Matahari—in progress at the China Television Station. Next to pop variety shows, historical dramas are Taiwan's favorite television fare, and with 5,000 years of history from which to select stories, Taiwan's television writers do not lack material.

華視古裝連續劇「西施」中的演員與錄影一景。古裝連續劇仍是當前台灣最受歡迎的一項電視節目。

The Taipei City Symphony Orchestra presenting Verdi's opera "Rigoletto." The Chinese have always been fascinated by classical European culture, which they see as the Western world's equivalent to their own golden age of culture. To the highly civilized Chinese mind, all human culture is interesting.

一九八六年四月，台北市立交响樂團演出韋爾第歌劇「弄臣」之前的排練。中國人對古典歐洲文化始終十分着迷。

Scenes from "Rigoletto," performed by the Taipei City Symphony Orchestra. In opera East or West, costumes and make-up transform mere actors into living characters. It would be equally intersting to see an American or European opera troupe attempt a performance of classical Chinese opera.

台北市立交响樂團演出歌劇「弄臣」。你可曾想像過西方人演出全台中國傳統京戲，又會是一幅什麼樣的情景？

OVERLEAF: A puppeteer and her back-stage assistants during a performance at a local temple fair. Puppet theater is a popular offshoot of Chinese opera, with the same characters, costumes, and stories. The Chinese love nothing better than loud, colorful, outdoor performances amid the "heat and noise" of human crowds.

前頁：民間廟會搬演布袋戲後台一景。布袋戲除了布偶華麗、形象鮮明與故事動人之外，另一吸引觀衆的因素可能是中國人向來愛看「熱鬧」。

Various youth delegations gather to participate in the annual Double Ten Day parade at the Presidential Palace in Taipei to mark the 75th anniversary of the founding of the Republic of China. The Chinese youth of Taiwan rank among the world's most dynamic. Consistently high performers in school, office, factory, and farm, they have 25,000 students studying in American universities—the greatest number of foreign students from any one country.

爲慶祝中華民國建國七十五年國慶，台北各校青少年學生代表齊聚台北市總統府廣場作大遊行排練。台灣培植的中國下一代子弟在國際多項領域中都表現不凡。

LEFT: A member of a high school marching band clutches the national flag as she waits to perform at the annual Double Ten Day celebrations in Taipei.

ABOVE: A delegation from a local boys school proudly displays the national flag at the Double Ten Day parade in Taipei. Foreign visitors often remark on the health and vitality of Chinese youth in Taiwan. The main factor is no doubt diet, but a closely-knit family life and no-nonsense schooling are also important.

OVERLEAF: Public buildings in Taipei are typically festooned with a colorful facade of national colors and auspicious symbols during the annual Doubel Ten Day celebrations in October. Since many major national holidays occur in October, the entire city remains colorfully decorated with flags, streamers, and ornate facades throughout the month.

左：台北慶祝七十五屆國慶時，一名高中的鼓樂隊員手持國旗準備表演。

上：雙十國慶中，高中男生驕傲地與國旗並肩而立。台灣的中國青少年所以顯得朝氣勃勃，應該與家庭關係密切及認真求學有關。

前頁：在光輝的十月，自準備慶祝國慶起，台北的公共建築都裝飾得美奐美侖，佈滿愛國標語。

Students in school uniforms line up during the Double Ten Day festival in Taipei. At left, they hold placards bearing the image of Dr. Sun Yat-sen, founding father of the Republic of China. At right, they make use of a popular Taiwan export product—umbrella hats.

台北高中學生在雙十國慶大典中，身穿制服，手持國父遺像，頭頂遮陽小傘，嚴肅中不失輕鬆的一面。

LEFT: The Presidential Palace in Taipei, from which the President reviews the annual Double Ten Day parade. A portrait of Dr. Sun Yat-sen and a huge national flag preside over the spectacle, which attracts tens of thousands of overseas Chinese visitors from all over the world every October.

ABOVE: Female military cadets march in cadence during the Double Ten Day parade. Women in Taiwan play important roles in the military, police, universities, and work force—and they remain the undisputed rulers of the roost at home.

OVERLEAF: Charming faces of China smile and laugh as they wait to strut for the President during the Double Ten Day parade in Taipei. Taiwan's feminine beauty is legendary throughout the Orient, and very few long-term expatriate bachelors here manage to leave the island unattached by matrimony to a Chinese beauty.

左：懸掛巨幅國旗與國父遺像的台北總統府是雙十國慶海內外中國人萬衆一心的象徵。

上：有「現代花木蘭」美譽的台灣軍事女幹部不讓鬚眉地參加閱兵。台灣女性多半均能適應職業與家庭兼顧的重担。

前頁：雙十國慶遊行行列中的甜美笑容。台灣女性之美，在遠東婦女中應屬無出其右。

BELOW: A "lion dance" street performance by a martial arts troupe is an indispensable part of every Chinese festival in Taiwan. Lion dances help dispel evil spirits from temples, homes, and other buildings, permitting good fortune to enter and flourish.

RIGHT: Businessmen en route to work, housewives on the way to the market, and children heading home from school all stop to savor the "heat and noise" of street festivities. Below, right, performers masked as pudgy children—an ancient Chinese symbol of good fortune—confer "tete-a-tete."

OVERLEAF: Fireworks burst in the air above the Presidential Palace (left) and the palatial Grand Hotel (right) on the evening of Double Ten Day. The Chinese invented gunpowder and fireworks for fun, and they never tire of playing with them. In America, Disneyland's much ballyhooed fireworks displays are all custom made in Taiwan.

下左：台灣每一項中國節慶中都少不了的舞獅表演。

右：商人，婦女，以及小孩子在街頭上停留，爲了看過節的熱鬧。

下：台北慶典中的有趣畫面。

前頁：雙十國慶台北總統府與圓山大飯店夜空上的美妙烟火。

121

LEFT: The "head" and "tail" performers in a lion dance prepare to wriggle and writhe fiercely to ward off evil spirits at the Kuan Kung festival in Kuan Miao Village, north of Tainan in southern Taiwan.

ABOVE: Martial arts adepts flail themselves with spiked truncheons during the Kuan Kung festival in southern Taiwan. They use special breathing techniques and muscle locks to prepare their bodies and minds for all sorts of grueling tests that never fail to fascinate the crowds.

左：台南北方關廟鄉慶祝關公生日時舞獅表演頭與尾部的協調動作。

上：歡慶關公生日時，武師表演以嵌有鐵尖的棍棒抽笞身體的氣功絕技。

ABOVE: Four exotic characters at the Kuan Kung festival. Each represents an historical hero associated with Kuan Kung, who himself was an actual historical character deified by the emperor of China several centuries after his death. In the Western world, gods created kings; in China, emperors created gods.

RIGHT: A youngster dressed in an auspicious costume leads a parade at the Kuan Kung festival in southern Taiwan. People from all walks of life participate in these festive affairs, which are usually followed by lavish feasting and ample drinking at night.

OVERLEAF: An elaborate wheeled procession of youngsters representing various historical heros is driven through the streets of Kuan Miao Village by the "A-Team." The Chinese have always attached great importance to children, who represent one of the top three desires of all Chinese in this life: longevity, prosperity, and posterity.

上：歡慶關公生日遊行行列中，四名據說與關公有關的四名歷史人物。關羽義薄雲天，死後數百年被中國帝王奉爲神明。

右：南台灣舉行的關公生日節慶中，一名服飾鮮麗、神氣活現的少年領導着遊行行列。

前頁：兒童扮演歷史各路英雄乘車在關廟鄉盛會中遊行通過市街。中國人向來以他們的下一代爲榮。

LEFT: The Shan Ssu Kung Temple near Tainan festooned with streamers and ritual objects for a major festival. There are over 200 temples located in and around Tainan, which is the place to be in Taiwan during major temple festivals.

ABOVE: Temple attendants preside over a ritual ceremony at the Shan Ssu Kung Temple. Though most Chinese temples in Taiwan have Buddhist roots, almost all reflect a strong influence from Taoism, Confucianism, and folk religion as well. Chinese gods are not jealous.

左：台南市附近的一座廟在重大節慶中張燈結綵，香火鼎盛。

上：台南廟中祭拜一景。台灣廟宇雖然多於佛教淵源深遠，却也有着道、儒與其他民間宗教的濃厚色彩。中國的神是不善嫉妒的。

ABOVE: Puppets on display in Taipei. The costumes, hair, and make-up closely follow the models of classical Chinese opera and also reflect the inherent Chinese love for bright colors.

RIGHT: Actors prepare to zoom off to a performance of street opera on imported motor scooters. Jolting contrasts such as this are par for the course any time and any place in Taiwan.

OVERLEAF: A crowd gathers to watch an exciting performance by a martial arts troupe during a festival in southern Taiwan. Thanks to the Chinese need for human "heat and noise," such festivals never lose popular interest and always draw big crowds. The "flavor of human feeling" is one thing that television cannot duplicate.

上：在台北展示的表演用布偶，富有鮮明的中國傳統京戲風味。

右：演員乘機車赴露天場地演出，是台灣常見的景象。

前頁：台灣南部節慶中，民眾圍觀武師的刺激性演出。中國人濃郁的人情味往往不是電視節目能夠充分表達的。

A worker stokes molten steel, sending sparks flying, at the China Steel Corporation in Kaohsiung, while a supervisor at right observes, catching the glare on his glasses. Taiwan now produces its own steel for ship building, the auto industry, and other industrial uses.

高雄中鋼公司的工人煉鋼，右圖監工的工頭護鏡上反映了刺眼的火光。

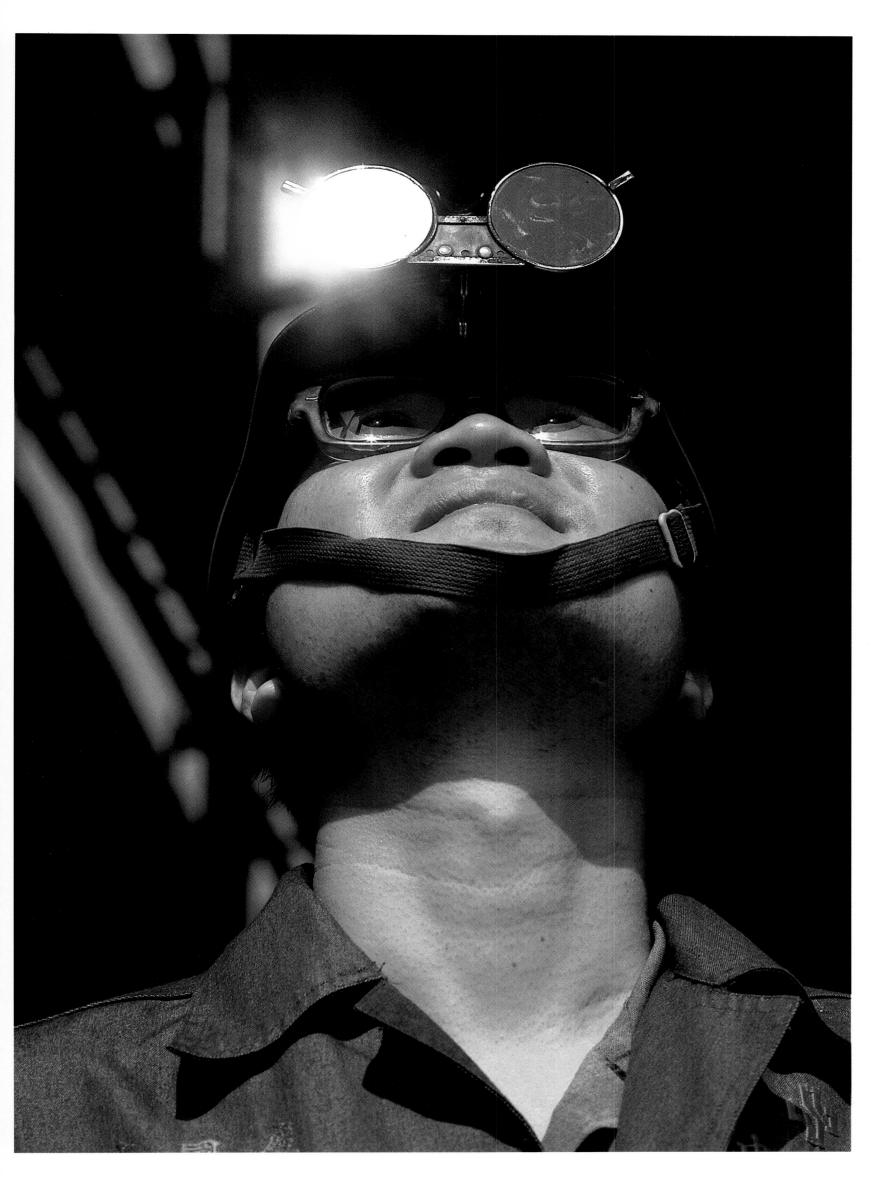

Workers inspect products on an automated assembly line at Multitech Corporation, a major computer manufacturer in Taiwan. Taiwan has already crossed the bridge from labor-intensive to technology-intensive industry and has recently created a computer that can handle complex Chinese characters.

台灣規模宏大的電腦製造廠商宏碁電腦股份有限公司，女工在生產線上檢驗產品。台灣工業近年來已自勞工密集轉型為科技密集結構。

Women work on sophisticated circuit board assemblies at a high-tech plant in Taiwan. This unit is destined for use in an American satellite receiver. Taiwan produces a wide range of high-tech components for the American computer and space industries.

台灣一家高度科技生產工廠中，女工忙於線路的高度組合。台灣為美國電腦與太空工業生產多種組件。

ABOVE: A poster with abundant cleavage advertises a new real estate development in southern Taiwan. With ever more money and leisure time to spend, Taiwan's residents are investing a lot of both in luxurious condominiums and suburban villas.

RIGHT: A man and a woman push their stalled motorcycle past a huge sign pointing towards a ship dock along the eastern seaboard. Chinese characters such as these forge a daily, living link with the past, which is renewed every time one reads them. The second character from the left, for example, means "to stop and rest." It consists of the symbols for "man" and "tree," i.e. a man stopping to rest under the shade of a tree.

上：台灣南部房地產企業以胸部線條豐滿的美女作宣傳廣告。台灣居民如今又有錢，又有閒，投資置產一時蔚爲風尙。

右：一男一女在東海岸通往船塢的路上合推一輛拋錨的機車，背景是泛舟休息總站的巨幅招牌。

LEFT: A woman caparisoned against the sunlight prepares to work the fields on a farm near the Deer Ear Gate Ma Tsu Temple near Tainan. Unlike their sunbathing Western sisters, Chinese women go to great pains to protect their skin from damage by sunlight.

ABOVE: A wizened old farmer takes a break in the cool colonnades of the Ma Tsu Temple at Dear Ear Gate, Tainan. The elderly are still highly venerated in Taiwan, thanks to the continuing influence of Confucius. The Chinese regard the lonely fate of the elderly in the modern West to be an incomprehensible tragic flaw of Western culture.

左：台南附近鹿耳門媽祖廟旁，一名農婦為了遮陽，「全副武裝」準備去農地工作。與西方女性很不相同，台灣大部份傳統婦女是很怕把皮膚晒黑的。

上：歲月滿臉的老農夫在鹿耳門媽祖廟的柱廊內乘得片刻涼。多謝孔夫子的教誨，中國老者今天仍受到應有的尊重。

ABOVE: A market scene in Hualien, east-ern Taiwan. Motorcycles have become the major form of motor transport around the island—and a major menace to traffic and air.

RIGHT: A woman in Hualien gives her grandchild a spin on her motor scooter. It's not unusual to see a 190 cc. motorcy-cle scooting through snarling traffic with a man at the wheel, a woman in back, and up to five children and infants hang-ing on for dear life.

上：台灣東部花蓮市場一景。機車仍是台灣主要的交通工具。上班之外，一家人乘一輛機車出遊的險象並不罕見。

右：在花蓮，一位祖母級的機車騎士，讓小孫兒也過過「拉風」的癮。

LEFT: A street vendor offers porcelain and jewelry for sale at the Jade Market in Taipei. Market vendors can earn a surprising amount of money in Taiwan, and many of them own fancy cars and expensive condominiums.

ABOVE: A vendor offers fresh apples for sale in a market in Hualien. Ten years ago, Taiwan had to import all apples. Now they are grown in great abundance in the cool glades and sunny slopes of the Central Range, where the alpine airs are particularly suited for growing this fruit.

左：台北寶石商場攤販出售的瓷器與玉飾。台北街頭小販一本萬利，有的據說早蓋了洋房，買了汽車。

上：花蓮市場上，果販出售新鮮蘋果。十年前台灣自國外進口蘋果，今天中央山脈山區生長的蘋果幾乎已有供過於求的現象。

A woman hawker in a Hualien market prepares fresh betel for sale. Betel is a mild cerebral stimulant and a powerful digestive aid and is very popular in hard-working, gourmet Taiwan. It grows on a tropical palm and is prepared for consumption with ground limestone and other ingredients.

花蓮市場上一名婦人在調製頗受中下
階層民眾喜愛的新鮮檳榔。

Girls giggle at a joke in a contemporary boutique in Lukang. Oddly, all mannequins in Taiwan boutiques seem to be based on Western models. While Western men in Taiwan invariably remark on the beauty of Chinese women, Chinese women usually extol the virtues of Western feminine beauty—and they sometimes try to emulate it surgically.

鹿港一家時髦服飾店中，兩名女郎笑顏逐開。台灣的西方男性遊客莫不驚艷於中國女性之美，怪的是，台灣服飾店用的塑膠模特兒莫不是清一色的「洋娃娃」。

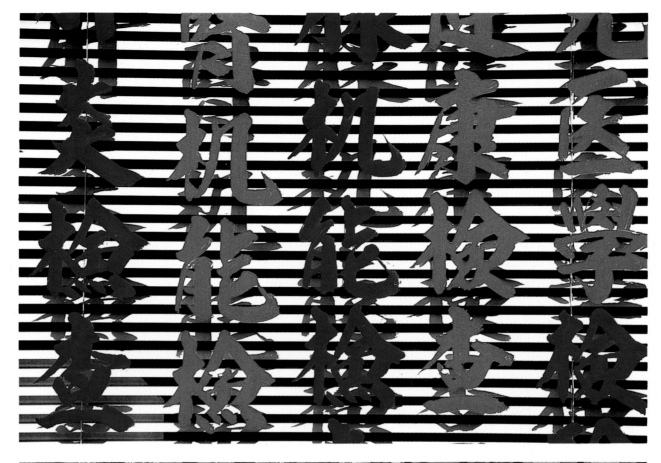

LEFT: Color dazzles the eyes everywhere in Taiwan. Above, a doctor's office describes its various medical services in patriotic red, white, and blue, which are the national colors. Below, children's shoes with auspicious colors and symbols on display in Taipei.

ABOVE: Young men smoke and chat near a school in downtown Taipei. The growing affluence of Chinese youth in Taipei has created an enormous new market for Western fashions, slick motorcycles, discos, fast-food, and cigarettes.

左：台灣稱得上是一個彩色世界：上圖是醫師診所的廣告招牌，下圖是台北鞋店展示的令人眼花潦亂的彩色童鞋。

上：台北市區一所學校附近，年青人抽烟談笑。台北年輕一代幾乎佔有了極爲西化的消費市場。

LEFT: A vendor in Taipei's "Snake Alley" prepares a bowl of spicey mushroom noodles, a traditional Chinese version of "fast-food" that tastes better, costs less, and is far healthier than American style "burgers, fries and a shake."

ABOVE: A vendor of exotic medicinal herbs puffs a local "Long Life" brand cigarette through a solid-ivory holder in "Snake Alley." Among the wares on display here are dried monkey heads, tiger genitals, red spotted lizards, deer horns, preserved wild rodents, and some things that defy description. All are tonic herbs with special aphrodisiac properties.

OVERLEAF: A clerk prepares an infusion of top quality Chinese tea at the Pu Ding Tea Shop on Nanking East Road in Taipei. This traditional method of drinking tea—known as "Kung Fu Tea" or "Old Folks Tea"—has enjoyed a big revival in recent years, and Taipei now boasts many exquisitely designed tea houses where a few pots of fragrant tea, some classical Chinese zither music, and traditional fixtures and furnishings combine to transport your soul to the elegant ambiance old old China.

左：台北華西街夜市以傳統中國式速食著稱。圖中女服務生正端着一碗可口的「香菇肉羹」。

上：台北華西街賣稀有草藥的，用一隻象牙製烟管抽着台灣製的「長壽」牌香烟。圖中展售的貨品中包括了風乾的猴頭、虎鞭與紅蜥蜴。你找得出來嗎？

前頁：台北市南京東路埔頂茶藝館中一名服務員正在冲泡上等好茶。近年來，由「老人茶」或「功夫茶」帶動的茶藝館生意一時鼎盛。

ABOVE: The Pagoda of Filial Piety at Sun Moon Lake soars against the sky, with bells hanging from the corners of its classical eaves. Former President Chiang Kai-shek had this pagoda built in memory of his mother.

RIGHT: An inside view of the Pagoda of Filial Piety at Sun Moon Lake. The octoganal design is auspicious in Chinese tradition. The views from the top of this nine-story pagoda, especially after the long climb up, are literally "breathtaking."

上：先總統蔣公爲紀念慈母在日月潭興建的慈恩塔，高聳入雲。塔簷墜着風鈴。

右：往下望的慈恩塔內景。自九層塔頂眺望，景色眞令人「心曠神怡」。

LEFT: The ornate, elaborately gilded altar at the Ma Tsu Temple at Deer Ear Gate, Tainan. Temples such as this cost a fortune to build, but there never seems to be a shortage of patrons in Taiwan.

ABOVE: A lacquered colonnade in the Ma Tsu Temple at Deer Ear Gate. Temple construction in Taiwan today faithfully follows classical designs, but instead of using precious hardwoods for the rooves, main support columns, walls, and floors, steel re-enforced concrete is employed instead, thereby saving dwindling supplies of wood for eaves, beams, icons, altars, and other parts which require detailed carving.

左：台南鹿耳門媽祖廟內宏麗嵌金的神壇。興建這樣的廟宇所費頗昂，但是在台灣却不難找到捐獻的信徒。

上：鹿耳門媽祖廟內朱紅的圓柱。台灣廟宇建築雖遵循傳統設計，但建材已多用鋼筋水泥以代替供應難求的木材了。

ABOVE: Typically ornate ceiling work in a Chinese temple in Lukang. The rooves and ceilings in Chinese temples are regarded as the dwelling places of the temple's resident spirits, and therefore the most exquisite craftsmanship is reserved for these parts.

RIGHT: Temples eaves, columns, and cornices in the Ma Tsu Temple at Deer Ear Gate, Tainan. Despite the extravagant overlay of paint, beams, tile, and sculpture, Chinese temples are perfectly proportioned and everything fits together harmoniously.

上：鹿港廟內華麗的頂板，代表了中國傳統廟宇建築的精華。傳說，屋簷與頂板是神明休憩的所在。

右：台南鹿耳門媽祖廟的飛簷與廊柱在在顯示了中國寺廟講求的和諧之美。

LEFT: The "Sea of Tiles" formed by the rooves of the Wen Wu Temple at Sun Moon Lake. In ancient times, only temples and imperial palaces were permitted to display this style of roof, with its elegant curves and sweeping eaves. Today in Taiwan, a specially trained class of artisans travel around the island to keep thousands of temple rooves and other parts in proper shape.

ABOVE: Tainan, known as "The City of Temples," boasts some of the island's most beautiful temple craft, such as this intricately carved altar. The most auspicious colors in Chinese lore are red and gold, and these appear most frequently in temples.

左：日月潭文武廟屋頂的瓦浪。在古代，只有寺廟與宮殿准許建造這樣的屋頂。今天，台灣有專業訓練的藝師，巡迴全島負責各地廟宇屋簷與其他部位的修護工作。

上：台南有「廟宇之都」的美譽，號稱有全省最美麗的寺廟。証之以這座神壇巧奪天工的雕塑，應該名不虛傳。

ABOVE AND ABOVE, RIGHT: A fantastic array of protective earthly and celestial animals inhabit the corners of Chinese temple rooves, keeping evil spirits at bay. At right, the mischievous Monkey God strikes an intimidating martial arts pose.

RIGHT: A goddess and her attendants gaze serenely from the ridge of a Chinese temple roof. In Chinese tradition, there is a close connection between the realm of Heaven and the emperor, who was regarded as the "Son of Heaven." Many Chinese deities such as the one pictured here carry honorific titles bestowed by various Chinese emperors.

OVERLEAF: Door gods protect the inner sanctum of the Wen Wu Temple at Sun Moon Lake. These doors and the guardian deities on them are carved from solid planks of seasoned hardwood. Note how Chinese deities invariably resemble magistrates in the imperial Chinese bureaucracy. To the Chinese, nothing could possibly be better than life on earth, so they hope and pray that heaven will be much the same.

上左，上：幻象般的人間與天上、負守護責任的珍禽異獸，棲在中國廟宇飛簷的角落裏，使邪魔不敢進犯。

右：中國廟宇屋脊上的女神與隨從俯視着人間的信徒。在中國傳統中，皇帝與上天有不可分的關係，皇帝也稱為「天子」。

前頁：門神守護着日月潭文武廟的內殿。對中國人而言，人間生活無比美好，因而祈望天堂－如人間。

崇祠隆祀典異代完人範古今
　　　湘鄉魯竹叢

勝景壯名潭兩間正氣昭文武

念大陸生靈塗炭金錢奮數同驅灰是渡河山

聚歷史文化精英廟貌重新共喜光華增日月

中華民國六十年十月

LEFT: An elderly Ami aborigine matron participates in the annual Double Ten Day parade. The Chinese call them "mountain people," due to their preference for living in the mountains. The woman's costume, beadwork, jewelry, and head wear are all handmade at home.

ABOVE: Japanese tourists pose for pictures with a trio of pretty Ami "mountain girls" at Taroko Gorge. Taiwan's aboriginal tribes are renowned for their remarkable beauty, physical fitness, and playful spirit.

左：年長的阿眉族山胞婦女在台北參加雙十國慶遊行。她的服裝與配飾都是出自自己的手中功夫。

上：三名日本遊客在太魯閣與阿眉族女郎合照留念。

Fruit farms (right) and fruit stalls (left) along the scenic East-West Cross-Island Highway. Thanks to the cool alpine airs of the Central Range, tropical Taiwan now produces grapes, apples, pears, and peaches to complement the pineapple, bananas, lichees, and other tropical fruit grown in the lush lowlands. The Chinese regard fresh fruit to be both highly nutritious and therapeutically cleansing to the body.

景色宜人的東西橫貫公路旁的果園（右圖）與水果攤（左圖）。熱帶性氣候的台灣如今高山上也盛產葡萄、蘋果、梨與桃子等水果了。

LEFT: Rowboats along the shores of Sun Moon Lake. Boating is popular on Taiwan's lakes and reservoirs. The great Tang Dynasty poet Lee Po is said to have met his death while rowing on a lake under the full moon. Drunk on wine, he reached over to embrace the image of the moon in the water, fell overboard, and drowned.

ABOVE: A sightseeing boat takes a group of tourists for a ride on Sun Moon Lake. The entire lake is fringed with a thick green collar of foliage. The lake itself produces a variety of carp unique to its waters, called "President Fish," in honor of the late President, Chiang Kai-shek. It is available, in season, at shoreside restaurants.

左：閒泊在日月潭岸邊的小船。泛舟在台灣十分流行。相傳唐代詩仙李白就是在一次月夜湖中泛舟不幸遇難的。

上：遊客可在日月潭租遊艇瀏覽湖光山色。整個日月潭環抱在葱翠的林木中。潭中盛產「總統魚」，是先總統蔣公生前喜愛的佳餚。

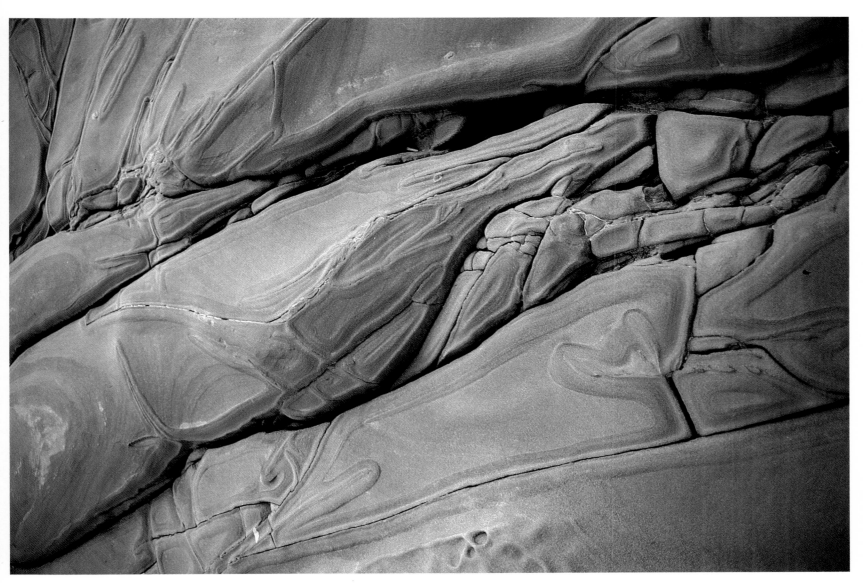

LEFT: Crystalline water careens across a bouler-strewn riverbed after cascading down the stone chute of the Dragon Valley waterfall at Ku Kuan, in the foothills of the Central Range. This river also yields abundant supplies of plump rainbow trout, which are prepared fresh to order in local eateries at this rustic hotspring resort.

ABOVE: Water worn rock at Chialoshui ("Joyous Waters") at the sunny southern tip of Taiwan. Taiwan's fiery volcanic birth left the entire island seamed with exotic rock formations, coral deposits, and hot springs.

OVERLEAF: A wave crashes on the coral fringed shores of Taiwan's rugged eastern seaboard and a timeless Chinese landscape unfurls along the East-West Cross-Island Highway. At Sun Moon Lake sunlight sparkles off limpid waters and filters into the camera through a screen of slender bamboo.

左：晶瑩的溪水，自中央山脈山麓谷關龍谷瀑布石槽瀉下，注入佈滿圓石的河牀。河中盛產彩虹鱒魚。

上：艷陽高照的台灣南端佳洛水海岸多的是長久經水冲潤的奇石。

前頁：浪淘盡台灣東部珊瑚礁緣飾的岩岸。許多遊客認爲這一帶的景色像極了加州中海岸 Big Sur 與 Carmel 之間的名勝。

東西橫貫公路沿途的美景就如一幅永恆的中國山水畫。這幅景色說明了何以這條公路有「寶島彩虹」的雅號。

陽光照亮了日月潭清澄的湖水，透過一叢秀逸的細竹，滲入攝影鏡頭中。在中國，竹子象徵了一個人的亮節與韌性，也是陰陽和諧的最佳表徵。

台灣之映象

敬致謝意
本書之出版承蒙下列人士提供寶貴之協助，特此敬表
誠摯謝意：
Mickey Chen, Teddy Chen, Margaret Cheong,
Chia Yue-Puo, Mary Crawley, Robert Ducas, Colin Gatenby,
Hwang Ching-Hwai, David Lee, Li Kun-kun, Joan Lloyd,
William Lue Hsi-Ming, Robin Moyer, Jack H.Y. Niu,
Rina Segal, Molly Sung, Tan Bee Choo, Sylvia Tan,
Nellie Tung Nai-Cha, Mike Workman, Yu Wei.
最要感謝的是居住在台灣的中華民國人民，給予我們
深植在台灣的中華文化特有的人情味。

本書圖片作雜誌、手冊與廣告資料之運用，請洽羅意恩出版有限
公司圖書室。
11th Flr Inchcape House, 450/452 Alexandra Road, Singapore 0511
Tel: 475 2033   Telex: RS 50634 LLOYD   Fax: 472 1690

Typesetting by Koford Prints Pte. Ltd.
Color separations by Daiichi Process Pte. Ltd.
Printed in Singapore by Toppan Printing Pte. Ltd.

ISBN No. 9971-84-897-X
First edition 1987

本書由台灣敦煌書局有限公司發行
中華民國台灣省台北市中山北路二段一〇三號
電話：五三七一六六六／五四一四七五四

圖：羅意恩 ・ 文：李丹

編輯：達偉思 ・ 翻譯：楊月蓀 ・ 設計：維詩康設計公司

　　Daniel Reid 的中文姓名李丹，是他在加州攻讀中國文學時，由當代名作家白先勇先生爲他取的。他給白先勇的唯一提示是他希望姓李，因爲他喜歡李白的詩與李後主的詞。

　　李丹在台灣一住就是十幾年，其間除了爲世界各地旅遊雜誌撰寫報導。經常環遊世界之外，偶而返回美國一次，回到台北總是搖頭感嘆：「眞受不了美國，看樣子我是註定要在丹鳳山莊作一輩子的台北通了。」

　　本文「台灣之映象」是他一系列──「台灣的影姿」、「台灣深入導遊」、「台灣的透視」──台灣報導中的最新作品，將由新加坡的 R. Ian Lloyd 出版公司近期出版。台灣之映象或許也是值得向我們自己的讀者介紹的。

由羅意恩出版社出版

本書的出版，作者與攝影師要特別道謝下
列的機構與公司給予我們的支持與鼓勵。

國立中正文化中心
國家戲劇院・國家音樂廳

中華民國行政院新聞局

中華民國交通部觀光局

台北國際會議中心

台北希爾頓大飯店

敦煌書局

亞洲化學股份有限公司

海灣包裝有限公司

福華大飯店

理成營造工程股份有限公司

諸羣企業管理顧問股份有限公司

美德船務代理股份有限公司

名程國際包裝運輸有限公司

恆蘭鞋業股份有限公司

福聚股份有限公司

優思秀股份有限公司

瑞士商西屋電器股份有限公司台灣分公司

古之欲明明德於天下者，
　　先治其國；
欲治其國者，
　　先齊其家；
欲齊其家者，
　　先修其身；
欲修其身者，
　　先正其心；
欲正其心者，
　　先誠其意。

　　　　　　孔子

"Illa Formosa" ── 「美麗的海島」

就在一五九〇年葡萄牙水手自澳門往日本航行途中，「發現」了台灣，為她取了這個名字；直到二十世紀中葉，西方世界仍稱她為「美麗的海島」。與鴉片戰爭之後被清廷割讓給英國的不毛小島香港迥然不同，福摩薩這個北起上海、韓國到日本，南至香港、澳門與菲律賓之間的國際貿易路線中樞，也是個富裕而美麗的標誌。英國、葡萄牙、西班牙、荷蘭、美國與日本都曾垂涎過這座美麗的島嶼，也曾費過心機要佔有她，然而最終她還是投入了她最慇懃也最具涵養的愛慕者──中國──的懷抱。

中國早期移民給她取的芳名叫「寶島」。台灣的土壤肥沃豐饒，她的山脈密佈了繁茂的樟樹、杉木與其他珍貴的叢林，她的山谷陶醉在不可或缺的生命活泉之中。

最初，自中國大陸移來的居民只是一股涓流：橫行法外四處掠奪的海盜、躲避種族迫害的客家少數民族與尋求暴利的冒險商人。但是十七世紀之間，當滿清揮軍南下誓志要顛覆並奪取明朝天下時，這股細流却滙成了大舉的流亡狂潮。在由海盜轉為愛國志士的國姓爺鄭成功領導的英勇起義之下，台灣成為反清復明的海上堡壘；三百年之後，在中華民國與大陸的中共政權作誓不甘休的鬥爭中，她再度担負起復興基地的重任。

「台灣」一名，是精於航海的太監鄭和於一四三〇年一次赴海外開拓，奉明朝皇帝命令將此一海島收入中國版圖時所取的。不過，有些學者認為這個名稱是「排灣」的轉訛；排灣是台灣一支主要且一度十分強大的土著民族的名稱，排灣族如今仍居住在中國移民當初來台最早居住的台灣南部地區。

儘管她有多彩的歷史背景與無窮的撩人魅力，台灣對多半的西方人來說，至今仍

是個謎。許多西方人將台灣（Taiwan）與泰國（Thailand）混淆在一起。（「喔，你住在台灣，」我老家美國的朋友常對我這麼說：「我聽說曼谷好玩極了！」）。台灣不為人知的主要原因，是政治性的：世界多半國家已與台灣的中華民國斷絕了正式邦交，使得這個島嶼在外交上陷入冷宮。然而她的經濟力量也同樣地製造了一種誤導或不完整的形象。雖然面積與荷蘭相差無幾，今日的台灣却號稱世界經濟成長最快速的國家、世界第二大貨櫃港口且躋身為世界第十四位貿易大國。人們一提到台灣，通常就想到成衣與網球拍、鞋子、插座、螺絲鉗子、罐頭香菇與形形色色的電腦，而不是她宏偉的山脈與翠綠的山谷，古廟與傳統的中國文化。

即使來台灣一遊，往往也未必能對這個島嶼有什麼正確的印象，特別是到這裏來目的純粹是作生意，就如在台北住了一輩子大約百分之七十的外籍人士一樣。除非事先對中國的歷史與文化背景有相當的了解，或者認識幾位住在島上的「台灣通」，否則旅遊台灣為你頻添的回憶大概不會多於在機場入境室短暫的停留。

到台灣來從事貿易或觀光散心，而不是不畏艱難的旅行者，此行所獲固然不出自己心裏有數的範圍：購買到廉價的製造產品，或被隔離在空氣調節的豪華巴士中四處旋風式的遊覽與購物。但是，能牢記「入境隨俗」這句中國銘言的人，將發現台灣是反映舊與新、傳統與現代、東方與西方繽紛對比的萬花筒，她也是古典中國文化的聚寶盆。自古廟瓦簷典雅的巍峨到摩天大樓管狀的矗立，從中國農業不變的模式到高度科技最新的境界，台灣向現代化世界猛力衝刺時，在在散發了世界最古老文明的晶瑩光芒。只要你願意暫時拋棄本身的文化成見，「伸出手掌來」，你必定會發現在台灣的中國人，會不吝敬贈你一份豐厚的見面禮的。

這份禮物是友情與坦誠、密訣與實情、直率與涵養的奇妙融合，中國話中「人情味」一詞最能表露此中真味。這種濃鬱的人生意味，在講求科技幾近僵硬的西方社會早經遺忘，家庭的情感聯繫與人際的友情常遭到邏輯與法理的侵蝕；而這却始終是中國人最重視，也是深植在今天台灣生活中兩類最緊密的倫理關係。洋溢在台灣各階層生活中的人情味，一如美味的中國佳餚，時時刻刻滿足並溫暖着你的心靈；然而，傳統的中國口味雖然在全世界都吃得到，傳統的中國人情味恐怕却只有在台灣才能品嚐到其中甘飴了。

自

地圖上看來，台灣像一片亮麗的翠葉浮在東中國海碧藍的海水中，與龐然的大陸也只是一水之隔。台灣寶島本身則像極了一幅中國山水畫仙境的複製縮影：蒼松點點的山峯與花邊似的瀑布，艷陽普照的海灘與濃蔭密佈的湖濱，還有巧奪天工的亭台寶塔，飛簷粉牆與古雅廟門，無所不備，却都天衣無縫地襯托、而非喧蓋了天然的背景。

根據中國民間傳說，台灣是由一條頑心未眠的海龍翻江搗海、噴着火焰，將海底巨石翻出而形成的。此一神話般的比喻倒是與現代地質學家的理論十分吻合的。他們指出，這個島嶼是經由有強烈火山爆發與地震將它自海底推出海面的。在台灣海拔二千英尺以上的山脈火山成岩內發現有珊瑚礦牀，正印証了寶島在殘厲火山爆發中出生的身世。

山脈是台灣的主要地質特色，覆蓋着葱鬱高山與熱帶植物的高峯峻嶺佔去了此一

島嶼三分之二的地域。從不輕易離開首都台北的人將錯過嘆賞亞洲最美麗山脈──中

央山脈──的機會，這個山脈的峻嶺不僅將台灣由北至南平分為二，也擁有東北亞最

高、海拔一萬三千一百一十英尺的玉山。

山脈也是中國人稱之為「山地人」的本島原住居土著部落的家鄉。目前人口大約

二十五萬的台灣山地居民在島上定居已有一萬多年的歷史，有九個部落在中央山脈四

處分佈的偏僻山區中至今仍保有他們古老的傳統。身為才華橫溢的樂師、舞者、紡織

者與雕刻者，山地人為台灣這幅織錦織上了繽紛的條紋。

台灣在五行中陽剛的火中出世，却受到陰柔的水行滋育並塑造了她的個性，有時

發一陣潑辣刮起颱風，會把全島整得七暈八素。世界上如果有任何事物能重振一個人

對大自然原始力量與風雨威力的尊敬，那該是台灣的颱風。

水，在台灣以多種面目出現。最鮮明的是島上的天然資產──海灘。其次是雨水

，全島每年平均降雨量為四十五英寸，而中央山脈高地的雨量更高出四、五倍之多。

如此豐盛的雨量形成的急湍短河，雖然偶或淹沒低地，却也繁育了為寶島風景增添無

限朝氣的壯麗瀑布。在其他地區，雨水也形成了悠靜的湖泊，譬如日月潭，就是台灣

最令人喜愛的蜜月勝地。

雨水滲入島上微燒的火山裂隙之後，經「龍焰」滾至沸騰，注入大地的生命礦源

，過濾之後噴回地面，就成了令人渾身舒暢又治百病的溫泉，這也是台灣最吸引人的

一個特色之一。台灣全島約有一百處礦泉源頭自地底湧出有治療功能的琉璜礦水，但

其中僅有十幾處全面開發為溫泉浴所，這些溫泉多半都設在高山中，四周繞着竹林怪

石，空中響着鳥鳴水聲。

台灣最普遍且濃烈的水份，是整年瀰漫全島、看不見卻摸得到的濕氣層面。這種

難得降至百分之八十以下的濕度，在空氣中形成一襲無所不覆的潤濕斗蓬，燜出了炎

夏的炙熱也渲染了嚴冬的寒意。這種看不見卻時刻呈現的水份，點出了台灣氣候中女

人味十足的特性，也使得天氣無比地難以預測。一天之內，溫差變化可達華氏廿度之

距。可能清晨醒來，天邊一片濃雲迷霧，中午卻艷陽高照；下午突然雷雨交加，淋得

你成了落湯雞，到夜晚說不定卻冷得你打冷顫。

如此難測且多變的氣候似乎強化了人類的情緒，也呈現了台灣傳統中國社會中最

突出的人情味特質。有時候，大地之母將這個島嶼緊緊地抱在令人昏眩的熱霧與濕氣

中，耗盡了島上居民的精力，衰萎了大家的健康，整個島像是一個巨型的蒸氣浴室。

在這樣的日子裏，特別是蒸籠般的柏油叢林台北，人們滿腔的七情六慾常不知何從發

洩。餐館、茶室、理髮館、澡堂以及其他有冷氣設備的舒適綠洲，滿足顧客的飢、渴

與他種難捱的慾望而生意興隆，大發利市；必須在街頭討生活的人卻是只有喃喃怨咒

天氣的份兒了。

熬過燠熱不歇，偶而還有暴雨與颱風作虐的六、七個月份之後，台灣在十與十一

月之間每年可以享有一、兩個月極為宜人又相當穩定的好天氣。更可喜的是，這也正

是海外華僑大學歸國歡度光輝十月慶典的大好良機。

之後，台灣天氣又開始轉冷。一如夏天的炎熱，冬天寒風中的刺骨冷意並非源自

溫度上的陽剛因素，而是濕氣中的陰柔元素作祟。這種季節冷得不單刺骨，而且令人

心寒。在幾年前的一個冬天，二月初就飄起了毛毛寒雨，據我一位朋友說，大概要連

續淋上四十五天呢。這樣無有盡止、又陰又濕的天氣，令我感到寒冷且意志全消；到

了第二十七天，我忍無可忍，背起行囊，搭機飛往印度南部，享受一番日光浴與衝浪板之後，在四月初返回台北，剛好又趕上了一個月通常稱爲「梅雨」的季節。這種四月及時雨，雖也是一年準來一次，却是溫順且稀疏的，不似冬雨那般刺骨而持久。

會

有人很適切地將文明定義爲「羣聚生活的藝術」。一個地區越擁擠，它的居民也越須擴充他們的資源，將大衆組織成如家庭、鄉村與國家等合作性質的單位。從這個觀點來看，文明成爲不可或缺且攸關生死的大業，而不僅是取代野蠻的精緻替用品。

中國人比世界上任何一個民族更早開始在同一片土地之上分享有組織的社區生活；因而，爲了生存與奮鬥，他們比那些人口稀少却享有無限廣土與無窮資源的民族，也更加「文明」。

中國都市生活的歷史記錄幾乎可以追溯到五千年之前，這使得中國人享有世界上最古老的前進文明，他們也是世界上最富經驗的都市居民。到台灣、香港或任何有中國人聚居的地區旅遊，最先發覺的，可能是中國人喜歡人多也挺享受令其他民族皺眉的所謂「吵鬧」。洞察力無比銳利的中國語言將文明生活中的擁擠與不協調形容爲「熱鬧」，中國人用這個字眼來象徵好玩、刺激且值得神往的事情。

中國大陸的「億萬人口」雖早已盡人皆知，但一般人却不曉得台灣的人口密度猶高於大陸。台灣的兩千萬人民忍受着（或許該說「享受」）大約每平方公里五四〇人的人口密度，爲僅次於孟加拉的世界人口最稠密的地區。人口約三百萬的首都台北市

，平均每一萬人分享一平方公里的空間。但與孟加拉與中國大陸不同的是，台灣居民

豐衣足食，經濟不停起飛，這或許多少也該歸功於中國傳統的「羣居藝術」吧。

即令在市郊，中國人也比較喜歡住在隣人衆多的所在，聚在高聳入雲的公寓大樓

裏似乎要比疏落的獨門獨院要好。隔隣的嬰兒啼哭、發火的太太大聲責罵丈夫、自窗

外射進的電視螢光或深夜家犬的狂吠……都被認作是人類羣居生活理所應有且令人安

心的聲響，「熱」與「鬧」正是文明的迴響。美國牧場或瑞士農舍、豪華遊艇或奢麗

套房中的生活，不知該有多寂寞呢。

在整個中國語言中，幾乎找不出與西方純個人意味的「私密權」同等的母語字眼

。所謂私密的觀念，在五千年羣居的歷史中，早在中國語言中淘汰掉了。最接近由英

語 "privacy" 翻譯過來的「私密權」的中國原有同義詞或許就是「自私」一詞了。換

句話說，在一個文明的社會中要求個人的隱密，不僅意味着自私，而且是十分違背羣

居生活的宗旨的。

缺少私密權的觀念，正說明了中國人際關係中，「面子」這個因素的無比重要性

。面子是中國人用來彌補欠缺個人私密權的社交技巧；在一個稠密擁擠的城市中，無

論是身體或心理上，都很難膽出屬於個人的空間，因而中國人學會了給人面子以代替

私密權的應變之道。面子有助於潤滑社交的齒輪，也減低了大城文明生活特有的人類

關係中因難免緊密接觸而產生的摩擦。誇大其詞的讚美與恭維，用來遮掩大家心裏都

有數却可能導致衝突的不愉快事實，的確是十分便利的巧技。別人在工作上遭遇挫折

或家裏出了難以啓口之事，中國人知道了，絕不會火上加油或打落水狗。他們或許會

與朋友饒舌不已，但是見了當事人的面，可要裝得一無所知。

台北是當今世界中國城市的典範，中國五千年都市傳統下的現代神童。身爲中華民國的首都，它也與其他國家的首都同樣散發着一股自視頗高的氣焰。但與其他政府首都不同的是，台北也是這個島嶼的經濟與社會中樞、文化中心，這使得這個都市的生活步調極具「熱鬧」，未開竅的旅遊觀光客可能倍感疲累，但絕不會枯燥無聊。

鈴聲四響的三輪車與坑坑窪窪的路面，違章陋屋與未加蓋的陰溝，在過去曾使台北獲得亞洲都市「醜小鴨」的不雅綽號。但打從一九七〇年代中期巨型高樓建築業起飛以來，台北有似火化灰燼中飛上枝頭的鳳凰，躍爲東方最具動力、成長飛速而且十分講求風格的都市。台北這隻羽色繽紛的珍禽，天景中閃爍着聳入雲端的摩天大樓反映了最時髦的建築，而蹲在下面的傳統中國廟宇，却綻出彩釉瓦簷玲瓏剔透的柔光。

流行尖端的服飾店中，雷射光芒配合着新潮音樂，炫耀了來自巴黎與紐約的名牌時裝；然而緊隣就找得到一家中國傳統中藥舖裏，一名峭瘦的中國藥師，在飽經歲月滋潤的檀木櫃枱上研磨人參、石膏與雄牛胆。城裏仍四處可見的露天菜市場裏，鷄叫魚跳聲中，買菜的與賣菜的高聲討價還價；走過對街，空調設備的西式超級市場中，却見顧客悠閒地精挑細選，將不二價、玻璃紙包裝的水果與早經切好的上等魚肉往籃車裏裝。這家正用筷子啜食正宗川味牛肉麵，隣家却可能在街角的連鎖快速小吃店裏大嚼漢堡，與炸薯條。這都是台北日常生活的一景，這個有如變色龍的都市，就像它的氣候，無需順應合理的預測與邏輯的標示。

台灣第二大都市與主要國際港口高雄，位瀕本島南海岸。毫不矜持地走在時代尖端而且堅守商業本位，高雄是推動台灣經濟動脈的馬達，台北則掌穩着舵盤。

高雄的一大勳績，是擁有世界最大的廢船拆除工業。拆除工人手持熔接用氣焊、

銀頭與鉗子在龐然大物般的廢船四下忙碌時，看起來就像渺小的螞蟻奮力地肢解一隻巨型甲蟲的殘骸。一枚螺帽，一隻螺絲釘，一個絞盤或一捲鐵線都丟棄不得，全可充作零件或航海文物去變賣。幾年前我在高雄街頭閒逛，路過一家專賣航海古董的店舖，窗口陳列的一塊雕鏤奇美的玻璃吸引了我的視線。隔窗佇視良久，我禁不住踱入店內仔細端祥。仍然認不出這塊玻璃哪點眼熟，我終於向店員打聽，他回答說：「喔，那塊是拆船工地剛送到的。聽說是『新阿姆斯特丹號』酒吧間裏的裝飾。」。我的老天！十年前，我曾在新阿姆斯特丹號加勒比海航線上充任社交指導，不知多少個子夜良辰，我一杯又一杯地淺啜睡前酒時，都曾若有所思地凝視過這塊玻璃嵌板。驚視這片經肢解的回憶，竟然在台灣一家古董店的一堆遺物中孤寂地棄在那裏，我感到莫名的怪異且悲涼；然而再往深裏回想，即令或許是象徵性的，這與我自己作客此鄉，卻也不謀而合。

這正是台灣──東方與西方，現代與傳統的折衷結合。不過，特別在台北與高雄，且慢被表面閃爍的一切華麗光彩給哄住了。在現代的粧扮之下，台灣卻跳躍着一顆頑強的傳統之心。一眼望去，現代感染力中的陽剛，似乎比傳統文化中的陰柔要鮮明，但是細心多看幾眼，你就會發現那給予中國人用之不竭精力的根深而古老的文化源頭。那種文化具有全然女性與唯美的本質，不似日本與西方那樣粗獷且氣勢逼人，卻含蘊了中國文明中持久、迷人與活力的密訣。

傳統中國文化是完成台灣這幅彩色分明的拼圖遊戲中的密鑰。文化使得中國人與過去緊繫在一起，讓他們覺得現況較易容忍，也與未來的捉摸不定有了隔絕。

文化也是中國民族誌學中複雜方程式的共有分母，因為中國人在種族上一如歐洲，相當的多樣化。事實上，「中國」這個字眼，形容一種文化，而非一個種族，因此，就某種意義而言，它意味了任何人只要接受這種文化，就可以成為中國人。

在台灣，傳統中國文化有兩個層面。較明顯的一面屬於感官與靜態的：博物館中陳列的無價藝術瑰寶，藝廊與店舖中的傳統繪畫與藝品，廟宇、山巒與其他古典建築，以及神壇到廣告無所不備的典雅書法。台灣中國文化中較含蓄、基本上卻也更可信靠的層面是屬於人性的：人們生活、思考與感覺的方式，面對這個世界的人生觀以及相互之間的人際關係。

中國文化與中國人的特性均可追溯到同一根源，用一個「道」字就可總結。「道」的淺意雖指「路、徑」，但是它的含義卻涵括了自哲學至物理、武術至烹調藝術、夫妻關係至國際關係等所有「天下萬物運作」的原理。一切屬於中國的，都起源於「道」，沒有此一強固基礎，中國文明的整個架構都會瓦解。

道的根本法則是，宇宙萬物自浩瀚銀河至微視層面，無不由兩種相反却相輔的強大張力即所謂「陰」與「陽」所推動。隨便你用什麼詞彙——冷與熱、黑與白、正與負、水與火、日與月或是最常比喻的男與女，最終，一切萬象都歸宗於陰與陽有條不紊的舞動。此一人生之道的關鍵，在於首先在特定過程或問題中認清陰與陽的存在，然後將這兩種威力與人性的實況達成最適度的平衡與和諧。傳統西方對人生所採行的方式，企圖以人力征服自然、正確矯正錯誤、「好人」擊敗「壞人」或其他二元論的兩

法來解決矛盾。然而，中國人對這些問題思考遠久之後，早就認識到眞理不可能在等

號的單獨一端尋求得到的，而是在兩端之間、兩極的平衡與矛盾本身之中求得。在中

國特性之中的許多元素內都可印証此一觀點，可惜外國人多半感到高深莫測，不可思

議。

道家哲學的經典，是文長不過五千字卻玄奧迷人的「道德經」，據傳是二千五百

年前與孔子同期的道家始祖老子所撰。這部道德經是今天世界上唯一最廣被翻譯的書

籍，共有一百多種譯本問世，其中單是英文版即有卅八種。一如它所含孕的文化，道

德經的迷人不僅四海皆然，而且是永恆的。

「道」的第一大前題是陰的力量勝於陽，即所謂「以柔克剛」。我們可用大家熟

習的水與石頭的關係來加以類推，每個人都知道再硬的石頭最終也會被水消磨爲沙土

的事實。同樣的道理，女人只要懂得以自己的溫婉包容男人的剛強，以似水的柔情撥

熄他的怒火，從女人的沉默征服男人的暴力。更廣義地說，和平的「祥瑞」終就比戰爭

的「悽厲」更具功效也更持久，筆桿強過刀劍，柔順者將承繼世界。也就是說陰力到

最後能勝過陽力。

當代台灣最能生動反映古老中國文化的，是島上數以千計繁星點點的廟宇。多少

世紀以來，中國廟宇內的種種幾乎沒有什麼變遷，而且即令台灣思想最傾向現代的人

也不曾中止去廟裏參拜他們的古神。中國黃曆上的每一天幾乎都記載了某種傳統節慶

，而皈依了基督的中國教徒也不時去廟裏向祖神問安，「以防萬一」。中國眾神心胸

寬闊，絕不嫉妒，任何人前來參拜，一律歡迎；中國神一如中國人，慷慨好客，廣結

善緣。

中國傳統對來世的觀點最富啓示性，也說明了他們在今世的生活方式。在西方世界，人們想像中的理想夢鄉該是一種「人間天堂」，西方的宗教也將至高的價值歸於「天國」。但是入世的中國人却將來世想像爲「天上人間」，而且把人間生活認作是所有世界中最美好的選擇。

眞該多謝天堂與人間祥和的共通，中國廟宇絕不是基督教、猶太教、回教與其他怕遭天譴的宗教傳統那般陰暗、幽鬱與靜寂的膜拜所在。中國廟宇開放、寬敞且充滿了歡愉的氣氛，活潑的歡聲笑語與呢喃的禱念，誦經融合一片。老者閒步於巧雕石柱與精刻菩薩之間抽煙聊天，媽媽祈神再賜貴子之際，孩童四下歡跳喧鬧，學生在寧靜的廟院裏爲考試猛抱佛脚；遇上重大節慶，中國廟宇中人們活動的「熱鬧」更是響徹四周。傳統中國廟宇中不時洋溢的狂歡氣氛，正反映了中國人熱愛人間的生活與盼望來生也能相差無幾。

傳統文化在現代台灣的另一相關性的反映，該屬相命了。當台灣稍嫌鹵莽地邁入高科技未來之際，相命此一中國最古老的學問，自企業大亨到計程車司機、電影明星到家庭主婦，在中國社會各階層獲至了前所罕見的振興。台北一位吳姓相命家解釋說：「現代生活爲家庭與工作帶來太多的壓力與問題，今天的中國人有自科技之外的領域尋求指引的傾向。在我們的傳統社會中，西方邏輯與心理學的理論未能提供解決現代化過程中諸多問題的有效答案，人們因而重返中國哲學的古老源頭以求慰藉與指引。」。

任何通情達理的工程承包商，在向傳統道教風水相士討教以決定一窗、一門、與奠基均須附合最佳天相角度之前，是不敢在台北興建現代高樓的。風水，這項中國古

老科學，能探出引導自天到地之間天體動力的無形「龍脈」，因而設定對人類居住最有利的方位。選舉之前，台灣一些頗有抱負的候選人，常請風水相士來到家裏與辦事處中，重新安排傢具、擺設，以招進最大量的運氣——當然也爲了拉得最多的選票。

科學，亦或迷信？中國人認爲這是個無庸多議的論題。不過，無論如何，這種風俗至少提供了人們欣慰與信心，也因而爲手頭的要務帶來成功的希望。

當涉及生、老、病、死、婚姻與事業等人生重大變易時，在台灣的中國人對由來已久之傳統的依循可是一絲不苟的，而且經常會產生意想不到的後果。譬如，台灣的孕婦，有時會在預定產期好幾天甚至好幾個星期之前，到醫院要求剖腹生產立即生下嬰兒。爲了什麼？爲的是麟兒能在占星家爲他們算計好的最吉兆的日子與時辰準時降臨人間。由於龍年被視爲中國黃道十二生肖中最佳的誕生年份，台灣的出生率每輪到龍年就會大幅度上昇，使得政府必須興建新學校與公共設施以應付此一週期性的龍子龍女出生潮。在其他十一生肖的年份裏，現代節育計劃使台灣維持了與目前歐美相近的低人口成長率。

結婚日期、開張大吉、合約的簽定、旅遊行程以及出喪日辰，均需按照中國占卜家的玄奧學理與他手邊的古老曆書來擬劃。凡事求証的西方人士通常貶斥這全是荒誕的迷信，但是許多遵循這些古老方式的中國人，却能同時在高度科學與技術的領域中，獲致超然的成就。

不錯，中國人就像他們的後學韓國人與日本人，能在現代世界中表現不凡，正因爲他們把科學與技術規限在頭腦與工廠中，而在處理心靈與家庭事務時，却能繼續遵循祖先開創的古老人性途徑。他們採用現代科技製造汽車與電腦，與建公路與高樓，

但依賴歷經時光考練的歷史傳統來滿足身心的古老慾望。這些傳統賦予他們所需的精神力量與自信，以期在這個可說過於機械掛帥的現代世界中出人頭地。

語言比文明中的任何層面都能更確切地反映一種文化與其特質，尤其是中文如此古老與普及的語言，大約自二千年之前就已開始逐漸演進成今天的形式。倘若外國觀光客能突然聽懂台北街頭四處可聞的中國人交談與喧噪，他可能對中國人相互溝通的方式始而感到驚訝、隨後會發笑，最終大概是讚嘆不已了。

不信的話，請聽：

趕着去上班，擠在電梯間裏，張先生向同事吳先生說：「吃飯了嗎？」。用英文說，其實意思就等於「嗨，你好嗎？」，但是中文的意思的確是說的：「你吃過飯了沒有？」。換句話說，中國人認為讓一個人感覺「很好」，指的是他的肚子，不是他的心智，他的早餐，不是天氣，他的食物而不是他的情緒。在中國文明裏，欲得人心似乎須經其腹。

一種兩千年來無甚改變的書寫語言是如何地應付現代科學與當代社會所需的術語呢？請看中國語文是如何地巧奪天工：中國文字中有了一個「電」字，為應付科技發明，就創出「電腦」、「電報」等等與電相關的術語。會飛的機械叫「飛機」，水與泥混凝在一起成了「水泥」，研究變化的學問稱之為「化學」，而研究心態紋理的學問就叫「心理學」。

許多現代中文術語字面的意義能一下子將你振入古老的時光隧道。我最欣賞的一些字眼是「矛盾」、「風景」、「馬上」、「玉米」、「火箭」與「水龍頭」等等。說中文的時候，你會自然而然地為最現代的意念配上古老影像的服飾，而中國文語不

斷運用古典引喻，也使過去永生不息。難怪中國人似乎從不感染「未來不服」之苦，

他們以大家熟習的古時影像繪出未來嘛！

人

情味始終是中國社會品質保證的正字標記，也是台灣傳統中國文化中最主要的人性精髓。旅遊觀光客如果能將注意力投注在人物而非地方、內在個性而非外表形像，你將發現台灣到處洋溢着這股人情味，而且通常會爲你留下難忘的印象。

以「味道」來描述人性與人情，正是重感受的中國人的典型特色。在台灣，談及人際關係與個人特性時，甜、酸、苦、辣等形容詞人人都能脫口而出。快樂與悲傷、憤怒與恐懼、歡笑與淚水——人類所有的七情六慾都反映在中國的人情味中，也是在台灣的中國人每天生活中最鮮明的色彩。

情感豐富的中國人，傾向於將強烈的情感傾吐出來而不壓抑在心底，這常令外國人驚異，偶而還可能感到窘惑。台北的街頭與市場上充斥了哄笑、口角與寒喧，但是中國人覺得這並沒有什麼。原因是，中國人認爲：心中若是積滿了甜、酸、苦、辣或任何「味道」的情緒，何不放出來渲洩掉，然後輕輕鬆鬆地去作事。多虧這種表現而非壓制情感的社會心態，中國人在台灣的生活，令人精神爲之一振，而免於其他抑制情感的社會因人類歡樂受到束縛而導致的緊張與神經衰弱的威脅。

人情味中的一項基本社交宗旨是，家庭與朋友永遠爲先，業務與政治其次。一九八四年，台北作過一項抽樣問卷調查，請全市各階層的居民按重要性依次選出下列生活項目中的優先考慮：財富、愛情、社交生活、工作、政治與家庭。結果，絕大多數

的答卷者把家庭列爲第一優先，依次是工作的選擇、愛情與財富。政治排在中國人生

活要項中的最後一名。

由於中國社會的焦點聚在家庭與朋友上，中國人自然願意與親戚及交往熟稔的人

作生意，而這種慣例却被偏重法律的西方人斥責爲偏袒朋黨、內戚的偏差行爲。其實

，中國人的方式不但在人情上很有道理，在商業上也很說得通。在其他因素相等的情

況之下，商業來往，朋友或親戚總比生人可信賴；何況，即使對方不顧家族或友誼的

情面，毀了契約或開出不能兌現的支票，對付自己人際關係小圈子中的騙徒，在權

宜與實際挽救上，也應該比對付陌生歹徒來得容易。

中國人的個人關係，以贈禮與感恩的禮尚往來，不斷獲得更新與加強。每一份贈

禮與恩惠，都充實了施惠者與受惠者來往的聲譽與本錢，因爲依禮俗，受惠的一方總

須投桃報李一番的。

這些禮俗遠比任何法律條文更具拘束力也更有效，因爲誰違反了它，誰就在自己

的整個關係網中引起不利的猜疑與公憤。在中國社會中，出賣朋友或親人比違反法律

更令人唾憎。對中國人而言，上法庭解決個人間的糾紛，是萬不得已的下策。這同時

也明白顯示，原告個人關係不夠，才把自己的私人問題扯到法庭上去。因此，往往即

令原告在技術上是正確的，法官却可能對他作不利的判決，因爲在法律上他雖站得住

脚，處事上却顯然犯了錯誤。

過份重視家庭、朋友與其他個人關係，在公衆領域中自然難免產生負面的影響。

中華民國的國父孫中山先生，在廿世紀初期領導全民革命時，費了好多年的苦心期望

能將中國人團結在他的民族主義運動之下，然而他也曾感慨地說：「中國人有家庭主

義與家族主義，却沒有民族主義。」。缺乏公德心的事實，反映在普及台灣全省的欠

缺禮貌的駕車陋習，有毒的環境汚染公害，排隊上車、看電影、上郵局以及其他公共

場所中的你推我搶，互不相讓。

這種漠視公衆利益的心態，並不意味中國人有什麼惡意或純然無知。它所反映的

，其實正是中國人十分實際的想法，那就是在公衆場合中，每一個人都算是陌生人，

因此無需像家人、朋友、同事與其他關係密切的人那樣值得特別尊重。基於這個道理

，在台灣有自己的友人或喜歡交朋友的外籍遊客將會玩兒得很開心，懂得依靠私人而

非公家管道的人辦起事來，自然事半功倍。

最能簡潔體現深植於傳統中國哲學與生活方式中人情味的名言，見於儒家經典

「論語」開章明義的第一句話。這部古中國有志治學問政的人均須背誦的經典開頭便

說：「有朋自遠方來，不亦悅乎？」。如此，中國文明的開宗至聖孔子很簡明地闡釋

了文明生活中最大的樂趣莫過於友情，友誼也提供了人們勤練最高境界文明藝術——

慷慨好客——的機會。

朋友來訪，中國人必定款之以美食、暖榻、餘興與敬重。不論朋友來自隔鄰或近

鄉，偏遠的城市或大半個地球之外，中國人認爲是他們的造訪帶給了主人快樂。盡心

地提供朋友佳餚美酒與一切所需，主人不僅表現了他是如何地珍惜這份友誼，也進一

步加強了彼此之間的「關係」。這種態度說明了在中國社會中必須作到慷慨好客的重

要性，特別是十分四海的社交傳統「請客」。

長期用腦過度的人，如果能與台灣的中國人相處一段時間，管保受益良多。台灣

夜市與其他夜晚消遣所在彌漫的熱鬧氣氛與毫無拘束的感官享受，正是消除工作繁忙

與絞盡腦汁之苦，暫將心力轉注於感覺、腸胃與其他可立即滿足的器官的絕妙偏方。

中國人白天可能比世界上任何人工作都更辛苦，但是，他們總能以享樂的甜美來抵銷工作的艱苦，以夜晚的歡欣來補償日夜間的勞累，對身、心的需要給予同等的關切。

這種重視人性平衡與協調的觀念，正是何以在其他社會早已習以為常，而在像台灣這樣的傳統中國社會中，神經衰弱與精神崩潰、緊張與沮喪、暴力犯罪與其他社會病態仍不多見的一個因素。不過，許多「先進」工業社會遭受的人為痛苦，實在不能歸咎於飛躍的時代或生命本身。真該怪罪的是人性的無知與對大自然的傲慢，這也正是全世界可以向台灣盛行的中國傳統社會學習的一個寶貴教訓；在這裏，人們不止盡情地享受人生，在科學、技術、工業與貿易等現代藝術領域中，同樣有傑出的表現。

在外國人的心目中，這種人生方式不僅新奇，或許還有些怪異，但是對中國人而言，這是唯一的生活方式。累積了五千年羣居生活藝術的經驗，台灣的中國人不甚憂慮未來，因為中國人視歷史為圓形而非線狀的，也就是說過去反映了未來的一切。

的確，中國人對時光的看法正基於他們的想法與生活方式，因此，我們以傳統中國人對過去與未來的歷史觀點，從事簡短的追溯與反映，作為本文的結語。

中文中「未來」這個字眼，有「以後」的會意，指的是將來在我們「背後」，是看不見的。在西方思想中，將來是在我們「前面」，可以看得到，然而事實上，未來是一片空白，沒人可以預測，更遑論看得到了。如此說來，中國人將未來視為「在我們背後」，是看不見的，這種觀點是十分正確的。

依照中國思想與語言來說，過去永遠擺在我們「前頭」。在中國語文中，「過去」的另一個字眼是「以前」，擺在我們眼前，而中國人卻細心地端詳過去，以反映未來

其實，不論像西方人一般面對未來，或如中國人一般面對過去，「時光與潮流是不等人的」。然而，中國人正視的是過去豐富而多彩的織錦，而西方人面對的却是尚未譜出的空白未來。

今天，中國人凝視海峽對岸中國大陸的所作所為，他們認識到兩千年前發生的情勢再度重演：當時秦朝（正是西方為中國命名 "China" 的來源）霸權，在焚書、坑儒且奴役百萬中國人修建萬里長城以暴政統一中國的秦始皇統治之下，蹂躪了中國的西北。

不錯，秦始皇在社會動亂與羣雄割據的時代中，為中國強立了秩序，在中央集權政府的威嚴下提供了邁向國家統一所需的嚴苛訓練，在短短廿年中極有效率地結束了二千多年的封建制度。然而，如此一來，他的鐵蹄却將中國文明的精髓踐踏殆盡，而且全然無視於中國古老的人性傳統。沒多久，中國人受夠了他的殘暴統治，不過一世，他們就擺脫了他的恐怖餘毒，將國家重新導回祖先開創的康莊大道。中國傳統文化的振興是由輝煌的漢代所帶動的，它將孔子奉為國家至聖，並為後世十幾個朝代立下依循的規範。中國人也以漢朝為榮，為自己取了「漢人」的名字。

漢人的文化在現代的台灣繼續發揚光大，在任何一處新的與舊的形象中反映了出來；如果中國人對自己的歷史認識正確的話，歷史不斷變遷的風向終將傳統中國文化的種子播送到它的原地，應只是時間的問題了。